First World War
and Army of Occupation
War Diary
France, Belgium and Germany

20 DIVISION
Divisional Troops
217 Machine Gun Company
16 March 1917 - 28 February 1918

WO95/2108/4

The Naval & Military Press Ltd
www.nmarchive.com
Published in association with The National Archives

Published by

The Naval & Military Press Ltd

Unit 10 Ridgewood Industrial Park,

Uckfield, East Sussex,

TN22 5QE England

Tel: +44 (0) 1825 749494

www.naval-military-press.com

www.nmarchive.com

This diary has been reprinted in facsimile from the original. Any imperfections are inevitably reproduced and the quality may fall short of modern type and cartographic standards.

© **Crown Copyright**
Images reproduced by permission of The National Archives, London, England, 2015.

Contents

Document type	Place/Title	Date From	Date To
Miscellaneous	2108/4		
Heading	20th Division 217th March. Gun Coy. Mar 1917-1917 Dec		
Heading	War Diary 217th Machine Gun Company March 1917 Vol 1		
War Diary	Southampton	16/03/1917	16/03/1917
War Diary	Le Havre	17/03/1917	22/03/1917
War Diary	Carnoy	23/03/1917	23/03/1917
War Diary	Carnoy Ref Map 62c. Edition 1 1/40000 A.8.A.7.2	24/03/1917	29/03/1917
Heading	217th M.G. Coy. War Diary April 1917 Vol 2		
War Diary	Carnoy Camp Ref. Map Albert 1/40000 A.8.a.8.2	01/04/1917	02/04/1917
War Diary	Le Transloy Ref. Sheet 57c. N.30 b. Central	03/04/1917	10/04/1917
War Diary	Bus O.24.C.5.3 (Ref-Sheet 57.C 1/40000)	11/04/1917	25/04/1917
War Diary	Neuville Bourjonval P.16.d30.25 (Sheet 57.c.1/40000)	27/04/1917	29/04/1917
Heading	War Diary 217th Machine Gun Company May 1917 Vol 3		
War Diary	Neuville P.16.d.4.2. Sheet 57C	04/05/1917	10/05/1917
War Diary	Neuville	12/05/1917	21/05/1917
War Diary	Neuville & moocots Bus O.24 Central Sheet 57.C.	22/05/1917	22/05/1917
War Diary	Le Transloy O.25c.0.2 (Sheet 57.c)	23/05/1917	23/05/1917
War Diary	Favreuil H.10.c.Centre	24/05/1917	24/05/1917
War Diary	T	25/05/1917	26/05/1917
War Diary	Favreuil H.10.C.Centre	27/05/1917	28/05/1917
War Diary	Favreuil H.10.C.Centre Adv. H.Q. C.10.a.6.0 (Sheet 57.C)	30/05/1917	30/05/1917
Heading	War Diary of 217 Coy Machine Gun Corps June 1917 Vol 4		
War Diary	Noreuil C.10.c.7.8 O-31-D-24 Sheet 1/20,000	01/06/1917	15/06/1917
War Diary	Noreuil	16/06/1917	25/06/1917
War Diary	Favreuil H.10.c.Central (Sheet 57.C. 1/40000)	26/06/1917	26/06/1917
War Diary	Achiet-Le-Petit. G.13.B.1.6. (Sheet 57.C. 1/40000)	27/06/1917	29/06/1917
War Diary	Mount Renault Farm 2 Miles North Of N In Bernaville C.5. Lens Sheet 1/100000	30/06/1917	30/06/1917
Miscellaneous	Appendix I Summary of Organization Work And Activity In Noreuil Section	30/06/1917	30/06/1917
Heading	War Diary of No 217 Coy, M.G. Corps From July 1st 1917 To July 31st 1917		
War Diary	Merenault Farm 2 Miles N of N M Bern Aville France Sheet 11 Lens 1/100,000	01/07/1917	19/07/1917
War Diary	M' Renault Farm	02/07/1917	21/07/1917
War Diary	E 4 b 50.99	22/07/1917	22/07/1917
War Diary	A 16 a 8.8	23/07/1917	30/07/1917
War Diary	A 16 a 8.8.	25/07/1917	26/07/1917
War Diary	Yorkshire Trench	31/07/1917	31/07/1917
War Diary	During Advance	31/07/1917	31/07/1917
Heading	War Diary 217 Machine Gun Coy Vol 6		
War Diary		01/08/1917	31/08/1917
Operation(al) Order(s)	20th Divn Operations. Operation Order No 1 217 M.G. Coy.	10/08/1917	10/08/1917

Miscellaneous	Disposition Of Machine Guns In Divisional Front. Appendix 1.		
Miscellaneous	Machine Gun Corps No.217 Coy		
Miscellaneous	Barrage Lines To Be Fired When S.O.S. Is Sent Up By Infantry. Appendix 1		
Miscellaneous	Machine Gun Corps No.217 Coy.		
Operation(al) Order(s)	Machine Gun Fire Organisation Order No.4. 217 M.G. Company		
Miscellaneous	Machine Gun Corps No.217 Coy.		
Map	Map Shewing Machine Gun Barrages 20th Div.		
Map	Maps		
Miscellaneous	217 Machine Gun Company Appendix 2	31/08/1917	31/08/1917
Heading	War Diary 217 Machine Gun Coy-Sept 1917 Vol 7		
War Diary	Proven Area (S1 Camps) Suez Camp	01/09/1917	28/09/1917
Miscellaneous	Casualty Report For Month Ending Sept. 29th 1917 Appendix 2.	29/09/1917	29/09/1917
Miscellaneous	Relief Orders I 217 Machine Gun Coy	16/09/1917	16/09/1917
Miscellaneous	Relief Orders II-217 Machine Gun Coy	26/09/1917	26/09/1917
Operation(al) Order(s)	Machine Gun Fire Organisation Order No 217		
Map	Maps		
War Diary	Stafford Camp	01/10/1917	02/10/1917
War Diary	Ytres	03/10/1917	06/10/1917
War Diary	Sorel	07/10/1917	11/10/1917
War Diary	Heudicourt	12/10/1917	31/10/1917
Heading	War Diary 217th Machine Gun Coy November Vol 9		
War Diary	Near Beaucamp	01/11/1917	05/11/1917
War Diary	Geauzeau-Court	05/11/1917	18/11/1917
War Diary	Railton	19/11/1917	30/11/1917
War Diary	Fins	01/12/1917	04/12/1917
War Diary	Ribemont	05/12/1917	06/12/1917
War Diary	Torcy	07/12/1917	11/12/1917
War Diary	Bandringhem	12/12/1917	19/12/1917
War Diary	Racquinghem	20/12/1917	05/01/1918
War Diary	Dickebusch	06/01/1918	07/01/1918
War Diary	Reninghelst	08/01/1918	31/01/1918
Operation(al) Order(s)	217th Machine Gun Coy O.O.No.2	22/01/1918	22/01/1918
Operation(al) Order(s)	217th Machine Gun Coy O.O.No 3		
War Diary	Reninghelst	01/02/1918	16/02/1918
War Diary	Blaringhem	17/02/1918	21/02/1918
War Diary	Esmery-Hallon	22/02/1918	23/02/1918
War Diary	Margny	24/02/1918	28/02/1918
Operation(al) Order(s)	217 Machine Gun Coy-O.O.No 4	03/02/1918	03/02/1918
Miscellaneous	217 Machine Gun Coy-O.O. No 4 Amendment No. 1	04/02/1918	04/02/1918
Operation(al) Order(s)	217 Machine Gun Coy-O.O.No 5	08/02/1918	08/02/1918
Operation(al) Order(s)	217 M.G. Coy. O.O No 6		

21/08/14

20TH DIVISION

217TH MACH. GUN COY.
MAR 1917 - ~~FEB 1919~~
1917 DEC

20TH DIVISION

Vol. 1
20. Div. Troops 6ot

War Diary
217th Machine Gun Company
March 1917

Mar '17
Feb '19

Army Form C. 2118.

217 M.G. Coy

SHEET 1.

WAR DIARY
or
INTELLIGENCE SUMMARY.
(Erase heading not required.)

Instructions regarding War Diaries and Intelligence Summaries are contained in F.S. Regs., Part II. and the Staff Manual respectively. Title pages will be prepared in manuscript.

Place	Date	Hour	Summary of Events and Information	Remarks and references to Appendices
SOUTHAMPTON	16.3.17		Coy Embarked for France. Strength 10 Officers 162 other ranks. Casualties Nil.	
LE HAVRE	17.3.17		Coy Disembarked and proceeded to No 2 Camp Sanvic. Casualties Nil. Quarters under Canvas.	
LE HAVRE	18.3.17		Camp Inspections & Kit Inspections	
"	19.3.17		Camp Fatigues. Remainder Arms Drill & Infty Drill. Repacking Limbers.	
"	20.3.17		Ditto	
"	21.3.17		Ditto	
"	22.3.17	11.0 A.M.	Entrained for Front.	
CARNOY	23.3.17	6.0 A.M.	Arrived Plateau Station Carnoy. Detrained and marched to Huts at No 2 Camp Carnoy. Ref Map 62 C Edition 1 1/20000 A.8.a.7.2.	

Army Form C. 2118.

217 M.G. Coy   Sheet 2.

WAR DIARY
or
INTELLIGENCE SUMMARY.
(Erase heading not required.)

Instructions regarding War Diaries and Intelligence Summaries are contained in F.S. Regs., Part II. and the Staff Manual respectively. Title pages will be prepared in manuscript.

Place	Date	Hour	Summary of Events and Information	Remarks and references to Appendices
CARNOY Ref. Map 62c. Edition 1 1/40000 A.8.a.7.2.	24.3.17	3.0 p.m.	Coy Inspected by G.O.C. New 20th Division.	
"	26.3.17		Coy tried Grouping, application and single shot towards Practices with 16 guns.	
"	27.3.17		1 O.R. admitted to 62nd Fd Ambulance with measles.	
"	28.3.17		A Section attached to No. 59 M.G. Coy. C Section to No. 61 M.G. Coy for instruction in trenches. Sections marched to LEMESNIL and BUS respectively (Ref. map 57 c. S.W. Edition 3.A.) U.4.6. O.24. central 1/20000	

C.G. Stephens Capt
Comm'dg 217 M.G. Cy

In the Field
31.3.17.

217th M.G.Bg.
War Diary
April 1917

Vol 2

Army Form C. 2118.

Unit: 217 M.G. Coy

WAR DIARY or INTELLIGENCE SUMMARY

(Erase heading not required.)

APRIL 1917

Place	Date	Hour	Summary of Events and Information	Remarks and references to Appendices
CARNOY Camp Ref Map ALBERT 1/40000 A.2.a.8.2.	1/4/17		Casualty, 1 Other Rank, of Section attached to 59th M.G.Coy, killed in action.	
	2/4/17		'B' and 'D' Sections moved to LE TRANSLOY (Ref map 57.C. 1/40000) preparatory to relieving 'A' and 'C' Sections attached respectively to 59th and 61st M.G. Coys.	
LE TRANSLOY Ref Sheet 57.C. N.30.6. Central	3/4/17		Coy H.Q. and Transport moved to LE TRANSLOY, arriving 6.10 A.M. 'B' and 'D' Sections relieved 'A' and 'C' Sections, 'B' Section being attached to 60th M.G. Coy who had relieved 61st M.G. Coy.	
Ditto	4/4/17		A Subsection of 'C' Section was posted in Trenches about O.27 in centre (Ref Sheet 57.C. 1/40000) on anti-aircraft duty.	
Ditto	5/4/17		Coy took over Machine Gun defence of YTRES LINE between V.4.b.3.7. and V.6.d.5.8. occupying it with 'A' Section and a Subsection of 'C' Section — 6 guns. These guns were placed under the orders of the B.G.C. the Sector but were not to be moved without consent from Divisional H.Q.	
Ditto	6/4/17		'D' Section ceased to be attached to 59th M.G. Coy and returned to LE TRANSLOY.	
Ditto	8/4/17		Coy took over defensive M.G. defence of YTRES LINE in divisional area from P.34.c.9.5. to C.6.O.12. a.o.6. (Sheet 57 C. 1/40000). 'A' Section left B bre	

Sheet 2.

Army Form C. 2118.

217 M.G. Coy

April 1917

WAR DIARY
or
INTELLIGENCE SUMMARY.
(Erase heading not required.)

Place	Date	Hour	Summary of Events and Information	Remarks and references to Appendices
LE TRANSLOY Ref. sheet 57C. 1/20000 N.30.b.6.4thd	9/4/17		(cont.) North Westerly direction to new Right of line. 'B' Section (8 guns) to be attached to 50th M.G. Coy and occupied a position to left part of line and 'D' Section here hurried up to occupy the centre. 12 guns in all were placed in position; they were under the Centre of O.C. 217 M.G.Coy acting under orders 5th Div H.Q. The Subsection 'C' Section formerly acting with 'A' section were withdrawn to Coy H.Q.	
	10/4/17		Subsection of 'C' Section on anti-aircraft duty at ROCQUIGNY O.27. (Ref. sheet 57C. 1/20000) were relieved by Subsection of 59th M.G. Coy. They moved to BARNDY Camp { A.3.a. B.1.2. } (Ref. sheet ALBERT 1/40000)	
Bus O.24.c.5.3. (Ref. sheet 57C. 1/20000)	11/4/17		Subsection of 'C' Section with its two 2nd Guards M.G. Coy on anti-aircraft duty at PLATEAU villdow) A.19. centaine (Ref. map ALBERT 1/40000). Coy H.Q. moves to BUS O.24.c.5.3. (Ref. map. 57C. 1/20000).	
	12/4/17		Reinforcement of 15 O.R. arrived at Coy H.Q.	
	13/4/17		1 O.R. evacuated to 13th Casualty Clearing Station.	

Sheet 3.

Army Form C. 2118.

WAR DIARY
or
INTELLIGENCE SUMMARY.
(Erase heading not required.)

217 M.G.Coy

APRIL 1917.

Place	Date	Hour	Summary of Events and Information	Remarks and references to Appendices
BUS O.24.c.5.3. (Sheet 57C) (1/40000)	18/4/17		Company handed over positions in YPRES LINE to 60th M.G. Coy and took over M.G. defence of ROYAUL COURT SWITCH LINE with 12 guns — 'A', 'B' and 'D' Sections. Move was done night 15/16th but relief was not complete until dawn 16th inst. The Coy is in these positions under direct orders from Div. H.Q.	
	20/4/17		Draft of 7 O.R. arrived at Coy H.Q.	
	24/4/17		Subsection of 'C' Section on anti-aircraft duty at PLATEAU within A.19. central (ref map ALBERT 1/20000) were relieved by 1st Guards M.G. Coy and returned to Coy H.Q.	
	25/4/17		Left flank of ROYAUL COURT SWITCH LINE was not brought round to run due North from N.E. end of ROYAUL COURT to canal bridge in sqr P.4.b.0.7 (Sheet 57C. 1/40000) instead of running Westerly to Western end of village and thence N.W. to P.3.a central. One subsection of 'B' Section was brought nearer to end of line and the other Subsection withdrawn to BUS. The Subsection crossing this new line in 24 hours were employed in what only occasional sections's initiative on the gun from a position in ROYAUL COURT and le autre in reconnoitering of target we might... whilst their companies billeted	

Army Form C. 2118.

Sheet 4.

WAR DIARY
or
INTELLIGENCE SUMMARY.

(Erase heading not required.)

217. M.G. Coy.

April 1917

Place	Date	Hour	Summary of Events and Information	Remarks and references to Appendices
NEUVILLE BOURJONVAL P.16.d.30.25 (sheet 57.C. 1/40000)	28/4/17		Coy H.Q. moved to NEUVILLE. Transport remaining at BUS. 1.O.R., motor cycles drafted to Coy, arrived.	
	28/4/17		Subsection of 'B' Section in RUYAULCOURT were withdrawn to billets at NEUVILLE. 'A' and 'D' Sections relieved sections known as 61st and 63rd M.G. Coys respectively in the main line of resistance flanking S.W. end of HAVRINCOURT WOOD, Northern part of line running from Wood at P.18.a.5.2. Westerly to CUR.Roy's in P.◉.17.6. and then N. close to and nearly parallel with road to x and D.T.36.C.0.9. Southern portion from Q.13.d.8.8. to N.E. end of METZ and thence E.S.E. to Q.21.C.3.7. (sheet 57.C. 1/40000). 'D' Section occupied Northern portion with 4 guns, 'A' Section occupied Southern portion with 4 guns. Relief was complete by 6.0 p.m., Line in future referred to as 2nd line.	
	29/4/17		'C' Section relieved 'A' Section in Southern portion of 2nd Line.	

A.Mitchen Capt.
Comdg 217 R.G. Coy
30 April 1917.

WAR DIARY Vol 3
217th Machine Gun Company
MAY 1917.

Army Form C. 2118.

WAR DIARY
or
INTELLIGENCE SUMMARY.
(Erase heading not required.)

217 Machine Gun Company

SHEET I

MAY 1917

Place	Date	Hour	Summary of Events and Information	Remarks and references to Appendices
NEUVILLE P.6.d.4.2. Sheet 57.C.	4/5/17		64751 Pte HEYWOOD C. evacuated.	
	6/5/17		One Gun 'A' Sec placed at Q.20.d.15.15 (Sheet 57.C.) to cover Right Flank of Division in BROWN LINE.	
	7/5/17		'B' Sec and 3 gun teams 'A' Sec at NEUVILLE fired promping practice on range about R.IF.central (Sheet 57.C.)	
	8/5/17		'A' & 'B' Sec relieved 'C' & 'D' Sec in BROWN LINE HAVRINCOURT SECTOR; 1 gun + team of 'C' Section Remaining in Relief Complete 11.30 a.m.	
	10/5/17		'D' Sec with four guns moved at 1.15 a.m. from to an old german trench Q.10.b.4.4. (Sheet 57.C.) under cover of darkness and fired from there from 3.0 a.m. to 3.15 p.m. during artillery barrage. Targets engaged were TRIANGLE COPSE and Sunken road just aft E. of it. Gun & M.G. barrage were to simulate barrage immediate prior to Infantry attack with similar object to keep German Observation balloons at their station while Cat 52 of 2nd R.F.C. attacked them, a total of 6000 rounds to the british. No german observation balloon could be seen over the divisional Front.	

Army Form C. 2118.

WAR DIARY
or
INTELLIGENCE SUMMARY.

217 Machine Gun Company

(Erase heading not required.) SHEET II

MAY 1917

Place	Date	Hour	Summary of Events and Information	Remarks and references to Appendices
NEUVILLE	12/5/17		'C' Section with 4 guns relieved 4 guns of 120 M.G. Coy in BROWN LINE from Q.21.C.0.4. to Q.27.C.5.7. (sheet 57.C.) the one gun of 'C' Sec's formerly protecting right flank of division being withdrawn into the BROWN LINE from Q.20.d.25.25. to Q.21.C.1.4. (sheet 57/C) Relief complete 6.30 p.m.	
	13/5/17		Subsection of 'D' Section relieved 121 M.G. Coy in BROWN LINE between Q.27.d.5.0 and Q.28.C.5.7.	
	14/5/17		New Positions for new Lewis line taken over on 12th & 13th inst. were sited & open emplacements; Rough splinter-proof shelters were constructed at these new positions	
			Subsection of 'D' Section relieved Subsection of 218 M.G. Coy of 8th Div" on anti-aircraft defence of CORPS H.Q. C.29. Central (sheet 62c) Relief complete 12.0 Noon. 67499 Pte SYMINGTON H. evacuated	
	20/5/17		26734 Pte MORRIS E. accidentally wounded by 4595 Pte WOOD while both were leaving revolvers ("stand to") at anti-aircraft M.G. position CORPS H.Q. evening at 8.0.h.m.	
	21/5/17		Subsection 'D' Section on anti-aircraft defence of CORPS H.Q. relieved by Subsection 127 M.G. Coy. Relief complete 12.0. Noon.	

Army Form C. 2118.

WAR DIARY
or
INTELLIGENCE SUMMARY.
(Erase heading not required.)

217 Machine Gun Company

SHEET III

MAY 1917

Place	Date	Hour	Summary of Events and Information	Remarks and references to Appendices
NEUVILLE to BUS O.24.central Sheet 57.C.	22/5/17		'A', 'B', 'C' Sections Subsection of 'D' Sections withdrew from line to NEUVILLE. Coy moved to Bivouacs in Bus. Coy went W and S 4.24 central. Company came under order of B.G.C. 60th Inf Bde 13th Div from 5.0 p.m. to purpose of move not given.	
LE TRANSLOY O.25.c.0.2. (Sheet 57.C.)	23/5/17		Coy moved with 60th Inf Bde 13th to BEAULENCOURT area, passing starting point western exit of BUS O.24.C.25.25 at 5.0 p.m. Coy arrived at LE TRANSLOY O.25.C.0.2. (Sheet 57.C.) for the night. 30784 Pte PEAT R. evacuated.	
FAVREUIL H.10.C.central	24/5/17		Coy moved to bivouacs at FAVREUIL H.10.C. central, moving off 5.30 p.m.	
"	25/5/17		'C' Section & Subsection of 'D' Section relieved 8 guns of 114th Australian M.G. Coy in reserve positions in RIENCOURT SECTOR. Relief complete 12.0 M.N.	
	26/5/17		'B' Section relieved 4 guns of 60th M.G.Coy 2 in front line & 2 in support on right of Flugel-Weg wacht. Relief complete 1.30 a.m. 27th inst. Coy H.Q. (a.m.) extending at C.10.a.6.0. (Sheet 57.c.) Moved thence p.m. to repile catering emplacements or defence lines on	

Army Form C. 2118.

WAR DIARY
or
INTELLIGENCE SUMMARY.

217 Machine Gun Company

Sheet IV.

May 1917

Place	Date	Hour	Summary of Events and Information	Remarks and references to Appendices
HAVREUIL H.10.c. central	27/5/17		Ref Sheet 0.31 - D.24. 1/20000 Edition 3. Positions for 4 guns '13' Section fixed as follows:- (1) C.11.d. 3.4. firing N.E. E.N.E. (2) C.11.b. 3.2. firing N.E. & to S.E. } covering each other's front (3) in Sunken road C.11.d. 1.0. (4) in Sunken Road C.11.a. 5.4. } to cover front of Nos fronts 4 to cover each other. Sunken road is avenue of enemy advance thrust & fanning up there from N.N.W. to N.E. No 4 has traverse from N.N.W. to N.E. These positions to be numbers 1 to 4.	
	28/5/17		1. Positions for C Section sites at helps formation C.10.c.9.6. firing S.E. with marginal traverse to cover valley approach to NOREUIL and with a fire command of Sunken road to the C.16.b. to be numbered R.1. 1. Position taken over by D Sub-section with C.10.b.8.1. moves S. & East to C.10.b.3.3. then W to N.N.E. & commands sunken road when firing N.W. to be number R.3. 1. Position sites for C Section sites at C.4.c. 2.3. firing up valley N.E. and from alternative positions covering crest at crossroads C.10.a. 2.8. To number R.4. 1. Position to be examined towards for Anti-aircraft work at C.10. a. 6.0. Positions (1) (2) (3) (4) open emplacements made & not suitable for (2) (3) in mountings or Anti-aircraft by day.	

Army Form C. 2118.

217 Machine Gun Company

MAY 1917

Sheet V

WAR DIARY
or
INTELLIGENCE SUMMARY.
(Erase heading not required.)

Place	Date	Hour	Summary of Events and Information	Remarks and references to Appendices
FAVREUIL H.1.D.C.6.7.0. Adv. H.Q. C.10.a.6.0. (Sheet 57c.)	30/5/17	11.0 p.m.	Subsection "D" Coy = withdrew to Coy Rear H.Q. FAVREUIL, leaving its Positions manned as follows:- R.1, R.2, R.3 & R.4 by 'C' Section 1, 2, 3, & 4 by 'B' Section. Of these positions emplacements are made for all but R.2. which is anti-aircraft by daytime & in reserve at night, tripods being at C.10.a.65.15. at R.1, R.4, but not yet at 2. Splinter proof shelters have been made. There are ramps cuts at all positions at R.3 which is being enlarged. of defence making not. Splinter proof shelters at all these positions, traverse at night these nests made of splinter-proofs & Coy H.Q. at C.10. a. 6.0. (Sheet 57c.) (Sheet 0.31 - D.2.Q. section 3)	

C.E. Stephens Capt.
Comm. 217 M.G.C.

31.5.17.

War Diary
of
217 Coy
Machine Gun Corps

JUNE 1917

Vol 4

Army Form C. 2118.

WAR DIARY
or
INTELLIGENCE SUMMARY.
(Erase heading not required.)

Sheet 1.

2,17/M.G.Coy

JUNE 1917

Place	Date	Hour	Summary of Events and Information	Remarks and references to Appendices
NOREUIL C.10.C.7.8 O-31-D-24 Sheet 1/20,000	1		See Summary of ORGANIZATION, WORK and ACTIVITY during period 1st to 26th June in NOREUIL SECTION attached as APPENDIX I.	
	2/6		'A' Section relieved 'B' Section, priests being met at 10.30 p.m. at unlimbering point at NOREUIL Crucifix. 1' O.R. Casualties.	
	9/6		'D' Section relieved 'A' Section. 'B' Section relieved 'C' Section.	
	10/6		4 guns 'A' Section taken by night to sunken road LAGNICOURT – DOIGNIES in LAGNICOURT SECTION in preparation for NIGHT BARRAGE FIRING ordered for night 10/11.	
	11/6		Shell hole positions prepared close to and S.W. of D. LAGNICOURT – DOIGNIES Road about C.24.b.48. (Sheet 57.c.) Operation postponed; guns to be withdrawn	

Army Form C. 2118.

WAR DIARY
or
INTELLIGENCE SUMMARY.
(Erase heading not required.)

217 M.G. Coy

JUNE 1917

Place	Date	Hour	Summary of Events and Information	Remarks and references to Appendices
NOEUX- C.10.C.7.8. (Sheet 0.31-D.24) 1/20000	12/6		Day firing by gun emplaced in Souchez road C.11.a.4.6. on SAMS SOUCI MILL U.30.t.25.80 (Map ref. sheet 0.31 - D.24). Telephone directly connecting gun position with O.P. No shortage of fire obtained.	
	14/6		M.G. placed at C.11.a.5.2. ceased to be used for Anti-Aircraft duty by day and was permanently mounted by day at C.11.a.4.4. ready for firing on German working parties at times seen from O.P. at C.10.a.5.2.	
	15/6		4 Guns fired indirect barrage from 2.53 a.m. to 3.8 a.m. barraging German Front line between D.14.a.20.85 and 65.70 and German Support line between D.8.c.75.70 and 80.10. (Sheet 87, C.N.E. and N.W. 1/20000) Positions were shell holes about C.24. b.40.30. Barrage was made in conjunction with Artillery Barrage, intention being to simulate attack on centre of IV Corps Front whilst actual attack was being made by I Corps on their left. M.G. Barrage was directed on German front line for 9 minutes, lifting to support line for 3 minutes, returning to front line for 3 minutes. 25,000 rounds per gun were fired. No retaliation.	

Army Form C. 2118.

WAR DIARY
INTELLIGENCE SUMMARY

Sheet III.   217 M.G. Coy   JUNE 1917

Place	Date	Hour	Summary of Events and Information	Remarks and references to Appendices
NOREUIL	16/6		Firing again carried out as for 15th but positions further in Sunken road, instead of B50 x (average dist.) S.W. of it. This on account of Zero hour being too late (3.13 a.m.) for guns to come out of action after the operation, if in chalk Kr.S. Firing began Zero + 3 i.e. 3.13 a.m. and ceased 3.28 a.m. 2450 rds per gun fired	
	21/6		Night firing was carried out, Harassing a working party by 2 guns placed about C.11.b.2.3. firing from 12.30 to 12.45 a.m. and 2 guns placed about C.17.b.2.8. firing from 12.30 a.m. to 1.0 a.m. Target Enemy supporting between D.1.a.50.15 and D.11.c.7.7. (Sheet 0.31–D.24 ½corn) 6400 rounds fired in all.	
	22/6		'A' Sec" relieved 'B' Sec" 'C' Sec" relieved 'D' Sec"	
	25/6		4 guns placed in Sunken road C.11.a.5.4. fired indirect from 12.30 a.m. to 12.45 a.m. 3 guns firing on HINDENBURG FRONT + SUPPORT LINES between Comm" Trenches U.30.a.4.6.7.6. and U.30.b.00.25. to 00.60. and 1 gun firing at Road Junction V.30.b.25.20. This was the while raid was carried out on Enemy was running S.E. from V.23.d.1.8.	

Army Form C. 2118.

WAR DIARY

INTELLIGENCE SUMMARY.
(Erase heading not required.)

Sheet IV.

JUNE 1917

217 M.G.Coy

Instructions regarding War Diaries and Intelligence Summaries are contained in F. S. Regs., Part II. and the Staff Manual respectively. Title pages will be prepared in manuscript.

Place	Date	Hour	Summary of Events and Information	Remarks and references to Appendices
No.(Sh? Gurecy. P. Sheet G.31-V.24) (1/40000)	25			
FAVREUIL H.10.C.6506 (Sheet 57.C.) (1/40000)	26/6		217. M.G. Coy ('A' + 'C' Secs) were relieved by 201 M.G. Coy. Relief complete + whole Coy present at FAVREUIL by 3.0 a.m.	
ACHIET-LE- PETIT. C.13.B.1.6. (Sheet 57.C.) (1/40000)	27/6		Coy marched to ACHIET-LE-PETIT. Lt G.A. WEBB struck off strength of Coy on reporting to 145 M.G. Coy as 2nd in command + that Coy. 2nd Lt D.K. BROWN taken on strength of Coy on arrival as reinforcement.	
	28/6		Transport of Coy marched to ACHEUX becoming Transport of 60th Inf Bde.	
	29/6		Company (less Transport) marched to ACHIET-LE-GRAND entraining there 1.15 p.m. detrained CANDAS exchange 3.15 p.m. and marched to Mt RENAULT FARM via FIENVILLERS and BERNAVILLE, arriving Mt RENAULT Ft 8.0 p.m.; Transport marched from ACHEUX 7 and arrived Mt RENAULT Ft 5.40 p.m.	
Mount RENAULT FARM 2 miles N of N.W. BERNAVILLE C.S. LENS Sheet 1/80000	30/6			

R.Stephens Capt.
Commanding 217 M.G. Coy

attached to
WAR DIARY
for JUNE 1917

APPENDIX I

217 M.G. Coy.

Summary of
ORGANIZATION, WORK and ACTIVITY
in
NOREUIL SECTION.

ORGANIZATION

During the period the 8 guns of 217 M.G. Coy were organized for Defence and Offence in the SECTION, 4 guns being placed at the junction of the Brigade Fronts to cover the Front line on Brigades' inner Flanks, and two guns defending rear part of the Division's Northern Flank, one gun protecting the Eastern valley approach to NOREUIL and the remaining gun being mounted for Anti-Aircraft defence with definite battle orders to follow in event of attack.

Day and Night Panoramic range cards were made for every position and orders given controlling action of the guns in event of hostile attack.

Observation Posts were established from which a considerable portion of the HINDENBURG LINE, RIENCOURT, QUÉANT & the country in rear could be viewed.

Positions were noted whence direct fire could be opened on the HINDENBURG LINE and a day firing position, connected by Telephone to O.P., was made and used for engaging working parties often to be seen from O.P. in & behind Support line East of RIENCOURT.

WORK

Plain open emplacements were made for all guns, Number boards and Weatherproof range card boards were set up and Position, Traverse limiting and NIGHT line pegs put in. Strong Splinter Proof Shelters were made at the positions and at Secⁿ & Coy H.Q.S.

Detailed Defence Scheme was drawn up and handed over to relieving Coy.

ACTIVITY.

A certain amount of day firing was carried out from Day firing position but observation of the strike of the bullets could not be obtained.

Night firing was carried out on QUÉANT on one or two occasions but opportunities were rare, the active patrolling & large night working parties on such an unprotected front line preventing it as a rule.

30.6.17.

Capt. 217 M.G. Coy

Army Form C. 2118.

WAR DIARY
or
INTELLIGENCE SUMMARY.
(Erase heading not required.)

Vol 5

Confidential

War Diary of
No 217 Coy. M.G. Corps
from July 1st 1917 to July 31st 1917

Army Form C. 2118.

WAR DIARY
or
INTELLIGENCE SUMMARY.
(Erase heading not required.)

Instructions regarding War Diaries and Intelligence Summaries are contained in F.S. Regs., Part II. and the Staff Manual respectively. Title pages will be prepared in manuscript.

Place	Date	Hour	Summary of Events and Information	Remarks and references to Appendices
MT RENAULT FARM 2 Miles N.J. N.m BERN- AVILLE (FRANCE SHEET 11 LENS 1/40,000)	1/7/17		Day spent in cleaning arms, equipment, Guns and limbers each morning. 3 O.Rs. admitted to hospital. 1 O.R. discharged from hospital.	
	2/7/17 to 19/7/17		This period was spent at MT RENAULT FARM in training. Four hours each morning were spent in this way (8.30 a.m. to 12.30 p.m.) and one hour each afternoon was spent for equipment preservation. The training was carried out in three periods:— 1st Individual training, in which special attention was paid to the individual duties of the gun numbers. The indirect fire drill stoppages, firing over cover, sweep traverse and use of fire & 30 yards range, were also done on the 30 yards range. 2nd Training of sub-section teams. Opportunity was given to exercise the N.C.O. for handling their gun teams and	

WAR DIARY
or
INTELLIGENCE SUMMARY.

Army Form C. 2118.

3

Place	Date	Hour	Summary of Events and Information	Remarks and references to Appendices
Contd	2/1/17 to 4/1/17		Training was specially directed to the working of the gun teams as units. A competition was organised on the range for gun teams in which each member of the gun team thus to carry out his own particular task and the final result depended on the teamwork working of the team as a whole. The four members of the team were Gun No. for the competition was as follows:- The gun team stairs from the Lewis Gun and had to come into action at the 60ᵗ firing pt and the gun being laid by the gun number entirely by compass & spirit level and elevation from aial - the compass bearing and gradual elevation from gun position to target having been worked out previously by officer. A belt of ammunition was also to be filled. Shots were fired for time and accuracy. The competition was very successful some teams on obtn'ing sixteen hits having 18 or more shots out of 20 on the target.	

WAR DIARY
INTELLIGENCE SUMMARY

Army Form C. 2118.

Place	Date	Hour	Summary of Events and Information	Remarks and references to Appendices
Corps	2/7/17 to 29/7/17	8:30	Section Training. Special attention being paid to hardly by complete action by Officers. This was carried on by means of action schemes. During the whole period the training in anticipation of the next offensive was in large proportion of the time was spent in practising in getting new offensive methods of different kinds fully in general. Every spare interval was utilised in passing new problems with as quickly as possible. Spirit and élan relentive aid and 5 map and clinometer, compass. Various methods which angle list, and the wind were practised continually and have to be learned to be given in length. No. 1 was specially trained to take the place of the various methods. During the afternoons recreation was carried on by means of cricket, rugby, football and sports, competition on runs.	

A 5834 Wt. W 4973 M 675 750,000 8/16 D. D. & L. Ltd. Forms/C.2118/13.

WAR DIARY
or
INTELLIGENCE SUMMARY.

Army Form C. 2118.

Place	Date	Hour	Summary of Events and Information	Remarks and references to Appendices
Mt RENAULT FARM	2/7/17		1 O.R. Discharged from hospital.	
			5 O.Rs returned from Courses.	
			2nd Lt R. BUCKLEY returned from course of instruction	
			2nd Lt M.S. HUTTON and 2nd Lt R. BUCKLEY returned from course in aircraft recognition	
			1 O.R. evacuated to Base.	
	3/7/17		Lt E.L. YEO proceeds on I Army Infantry Course	
	4/7/17		1 O.R. Discharged from hospital.	
			4 O.Rs proceeded to Div.nl Signal School.	
			Capt C.G. STEPHENS O.C. Coy offg Divisional Machine Gun Officer	
	5/7/17		1 O.R. returned from C.C.S.	
			1 O.R. returned to Cookery Course	
	6/7/17		1 O.R. admitted to Hospital.	
	7/7/17		Inspection of B Coy by G.O.C. 20th Div. by Major G. T.G. MATHESON	
	8/7/17		4 O.Rs proceeded to 3rd Army Rest Camp.	
			1 O.R. admitted to hospital.	
	9/7/17		1 O.R. admitted to hospital	
			2 O.Rs evacuated to C.C.S.	

Army Form C. 2118.

WAR DIARY
or
INTELLIGENCE SUMMARY.
(Erase heading not required.)

Instructions regarding War Diaries and Intelligence Summaries are contained in F.S. Regs., Part II. and the Staff Manual respectively. Title pages will be prepared in manuscript.

Place	Date	Hour	Summary of Events and Information	Remarks and references to Appendices
Mt DENNIS POST	10/11/17		2 O.R. admitted to Hospital. 1 O.R. discharged from Hospital. 2 O.R. evacuated to 3rd Can. Stat. Hosp.	
	11/11/17		2Lt E.E. MALSCH returns from leave in recognition of aircraft.	
			1 O.R. admitted to Hospital	
			1 O.R. proceeds on leave to U.K.	
			3 O.Rs evacuated to 3rd Can. Stat. Hosp.	
	13/11/17		2Lt R.J. WHEELER joins the Corps for duty.	
	14/11/17		1 O.R. evacuated to G.S. Can. Stat. Hosp.	
			1 O.R. " to Base Depot	
	15/11/17		2Lt M.S. HUTTON proceeds to II Corps Infantry Course	
			2 O.Rs evacuated to 3rd Can. Stat. Hosp.	
			1 O.R. discharged from hospital	
	16/11/17		2 O.Rs evacuated to 3rd Can. Stat. Hosp.	
			2 O.R. discharged from Hospital	
	17/11/17		3 O.Rs evacuated to 3rd Can. Stat. Hosp.	
			4 O.R. proceed from Div Signal School	
	18/11/17		1 O.R. proceeds to U.K. on Corps Cadet School	

WAR DIARY
or
INTELLIGENCE SUMMARY.

(Erase heading not required.)

Army Form C. 2118.

Place	Date	Hour	Summary of Events and Information	Remarks and references to Appendices
Mt KEMMEL FARM	20/7/17	3 a.m	Thing moved off from Mt KEMMEL FARM to DOULLENS (N STATION) about 10½ miles march. Route: LE MEILLARD, MÉZEROLLES	Regt LENS 11/1/1000
		8 a.m	Arrived at DOULLENS Entrained	
		11.19 p.m	Train left DOULLENS	
		5 p.m	Arrived at GODEWAERSVELDE (Reg HAZEBROUCK on Hoogan). Stayed night here	
		6.30 p.m	Marched to WATOU to E6.c.28.25 (Ref BELGIAN Sheet 27) 25 Tents in Camp.	
	21/7/17 1.30 pm		Moved to new camp at E.4.d.50.99 (R/a BELGIUM Sheet 27).	
E4450.99	22/7/17		Day spent in preparing stores & equipment for action. 1 O.R. joined for Duty. Evac. 3 OR to Hospital.	
Alba S.P	23/7/17 1.30 pm		Struck camp and marched to Alba S.P (DRAGON CAMP) in PROVEN and situated N of POPERINGHE were at 6 p.m. 3 Tents to Officers. 1 Coy attached to 38th Div for operations. in Huts.	
			Capt C.G. STEPHENS (OC coy) slightly wounded while Reconnoitring line. 87 RA LDNS Scot Guards commanding party 1 Officer + 32 O.Rs of 10th RB attached to Coy in Laying party.	
	24/7/17		Lieut BEAUMONT by Coy Officers and positions for 16 guns sites in front of YORKSHIRE Tr. From C.13.a.5.5 to C.7.c.55.45 (LANGEMARCK (BOGERS) Sheet 20 . 28 Edit 2	
			2 O.R.S for Canada to Corps Rest Station.	

Army Form C. 2118.

WAR DIARY
or
INTELLIGENCE SUMMARY

(Erase heading not required.)

Instructions regarding War Diaries and Intelligence Summaries are contained in F. S. Regs., Part II. and the Staff Manual respectively. Title pages will be prepared in manuscript.

Place	Date	Hour	Summary of Events and Information	Remarks and references to Appendices
A/c. S.S	26/11/17		1 O.R. discharged from Hospital	
			L.O.R. Reynolds (injured) Coy from 3rd Army Rest Camp	
			Capt. C.G. STEPHENS returned Coy from 4th C.C.S. and took over command	
	27/11/17	10 a.m.	2Lt T. JOHNSON wounded by shell returning from Trenches and evacuated (since reports died of wounds)	
			245 7.S. BALL rejoined Coy from Machine Gun Course at CAMIERS	
			30 R returned from " " " " at CAMIERS	
	28/11/17		1 O.R. proceeded to Musketry Guy Course at CAMIERS	
			1 O.R. returned from leave to U.K.	
			1 L.R. admitted to Hospital	
	29/11/17	6 p.m.	1 O.R. admitted to Hospital	
			Coy. with Transport marched to trenches and put into YORKSHIRE TRENCH and HARKNESS AV.	
			Coy. only on camp	
	29/11/17	6 a.m.	Coy. returned to camp	
			2 O.R. admitted to Hospital	
			20 R. wounded at C.C.S.	
			2 O.R. discharged from Hospital	
			1 O.R. returned missing	
	9.30 p.m.		Coy. moved to a factory	

WAR DIARY
or
INTELLIGENCE SUMMARY

Army Form C. 2118.

Place	Date	Hour	Summary of Events and Information	Remarks and references to Appendices
Abaele	25/7/19	5pm	Coy reverted to YORKSHIRE TR. to dig emplacements on positions also on previous day. Work completed at 4 a.m. Sections on following C.O. action. During night B Coy C.D.A.B. Positions 25 in front of track and were sited in open ground in front of No 1 and No 2. The other trenches were dug to give protection to men sited in general old trench 10' to 15" in position of new YORKSHIRE TRENCH. Ran son as digging times from B new trench carried up from debris for positions complete ammunition dump. 54,000 rounds S.A.A. was left behind to took after during dump B Cpl ___ was to man the night was intermittent and positions. Hostile shelling during the night was casualties were suffered 1 O.R. A.S.B.S. Coy returned to ___ A.S.B.S. 1 O.R. admitted to hospital 1 O.R. discharged from hospital.	(4pm to 3am)
"	26/7/19	5pm	Coy under 2Lt T. JOHNSON and 2Lt R.J. WHEELER proceeded to line of track carrying ammunition. Return during B Coy was on duty chiefly along HARNESS AVENUE, communication trench leading up to YORKSHIRE TRENCH. 2Lt T. JOHNSON reported to return journey (feet) and wounded.	

Army Form C. 2118.

WAR DIARY
or
INTELLIGENCE SUMMARY
(Erase heading not required.)

Place	Date	Hour	Summary of Events and Information	Remarks and references to Appendices
YORKSHIRE TRENCH	31/7/17	3.50 a.m 4.12 a.m	Zero hour. Coy got 16 guns into action in front of YORKSHIRE TRENCH ready to open fire on barrage line C26.b.16 C9a.25.60 (Rifle LANGEMARCK YPRES) on S.O.S. call. Capt. C.G. STEPHENS in Command of Coy 2LT R.J. WHEELER commanding "B". 2LT R.J. BUCKLEY "A" section, 2LT D.K. BROWN "C" Section, 2LT E.C. MALSCH Direction.	
		6.2 a.m	Fire opened to support our attack on second objective (Line through N.E. end of PILCKEM to JOLIE FARM) on targets C26.b.5 to C26.b.9 and C3.c 16 to C3.c 7.0. Fire continued until 5.30 a.m. by 8 guns at rate of 100 rounds per min. The former 8 guns lifted to target C3.a.60.15 to C3.a.1.57 at 5.19 a.m. and fired on this target at a rate of 60 rounds per minute until 7.12 a.m. The latter 8 guns lifted to target U26.d.6.3 to C3.a.35.65 at 5.32 a.m. and fired on this target until 7.12 a.m. at rate of 50 rounds per minute. During this period 2LT R.J. WHEELER and 4 O.R's were slightly wounded by hostile shelling. This shelling was comparatively light but continuous.	
		7.62 a.m	16 Rdk. mules were brought by 2LT M.L. WILSON to junction of ALMA TRENCH and HUDDLESTON ROAD when fresh supplies of guns, tripods and ammunition were loaded on these. The Coy advanced by sections to the late of position M.LCKEM and IRON CROSS. Capt. C.G. STEPHENS and 2LT M.L. WILSON went forward to reconnaître and chose line between C2.d.9.8 and C3.a.25.05.	

WAR DIARY
or
INTELLIGENCE SUMMARY
(Erase heading not required.)

Army Form C. 2118.

Place	Date	Hour	Summary of Events and Information	Remarks and references to Appendices
During Advance	31/7/17	11 a.m.	Guns were detached along the line and had various on road running in front of LANGEMARCK from U22.c.90.35. to U28.d.9.6. Road was obtained with 154th Inf Brigade, the information that the advance was many troops in LANGEMARCK and that a counter attack was imminent. S.O.S. signals were sent up at 2.45 p.m. and fire was opened from 15 guns. (One had been left behind owing to difficulties of transport). The counter attack was beaten off and went on as 9 p.m. was also unsuccessful. During the advance the ground was very heavy owing to previous rain and guns had difficulty in getting the mules forward. One obtained itself so badly that it had to be shot. The Coy bivouacked on the ground during the night. Total Casualties during the day 2 Officers 15 O.Rs. wounded. Capt. C.G. Stephens was wounded about 4.30 p.m. and was sent down to Essex Farm.	

R.A. Kennedy
O.C. 207 M.G. Coy.

Vol 6

War Diary

217 Machine Gun Coy

Army Form C. 2118.

WAR DIARY
or
INTELLIGENCE SUMMARY.
(Erase heading not required.)

Instructions regarding War Diaries and Intelligence Summaries are contained in F. S. Regs., Part II. and the Staff Manual respectively. Title pages will be prepared in manuscript.

Place	Date	Hour	Summary of Events and Information	Remarks and references to Appendices
	1/8/17		Company near H.Q. at A.16.a.88, and Company still in line (DRAGOON CAMP)	Bdy. Shoot 2.55 W. /15.000
	2/8/17		I.O.R. wounded	
	3/8/17		I.O.R. guard. Company arrived back from line about 5 p.m.	
	4/8/17		2/Lt T. JOHNSON died at 46th C.C.S. from multiple wounds received on July 27th. 20th Divison commenced relieving the 38th Division in the line in the morning.	
	6/8/17		2/Lt A. R. METRAM joined the Company	
	7/8/17		59th Infantry Brigade commenced relieving the 61st Infantry Brigade in the line. I.O.R. reported killed	
	10/8/17		Company left for line at 5 p.m. to take over the machine gun defence of the Divisional front, relieving 2 sections of	
	11/8/17		No. 60th M.G. Company + 2 sections of the 61st M.G. Company in the line.	
			The 59th Infantry Brigade attacked this line across the STEENBEEK at 4.15 a.m. + established front approximately 200 yards east of the stream in conjunction with similar operations by the Brigade on the left. The 59th Infantry Brigade issued the STEENBEEK and consolidated the position on the east bank of the stream, + was relieved that night (11/12) by the 60th + 61st Infantry Brigades —	For dispositions see App. (attached)
	14/8/17		The Company was relieved on the night of 14/15 by 2 sections of the 61st M.G. Company in the left sub-sector of the 60th M.G. Company, of the 60th M.G. Company in the right sub-sector + 2 sections of the 61st M.G. Company in the right sub-sector (MALAKOFF FARM AREA) arriving back at camp (MALAKOFF FARM AREA) at 5 a.m. on the 15th inst. 2 O.R: Killed, 5 wounded. 1 gassed.	
	15/8/17		Company left camp at 7.30 p.m. for having position preparatory to the attack by the XIV Corps. 3.O.R: missing.	For instructions see: M.G. Instructions (Attack)
			The XIV Corps, with 20th Division on the right + the 29th Division on the left attacked LANGEMARCK at H 4.5 a.m. 16/8/17 (The Guards + 38th Divisions being on Corps reserve, the Guards in rear of the 20th Division + the 38th in rear	Orders by LT.R.A W192
	16/8/17		of the 20th Division.) The 20th Division attacked with the 60th Brigade on the right + 61st Brigade on the left with the 59th Brigade in support	O.O. N°1 20/7/17 DATED 14/8/17

Signed for Commanding 217. m.g. Coy

A5834 Wt. W4973/M687 750,000 8/16 D. D. & L. Ltd. Forms/C.2113/13.

WAR DIARY
or
INTELLIGENCE SUMMARY
(Erase heading not required.)

Army Form C. 2118.

Place	Date	Hour	Summary of Events and Information	Remarks and references to Appendices
	16/8/17		2/Lt A.R. Mettam killed. Lt R.A. Lumb (Commanding) 2/Lt C.S. Ball wounded. 2/Lt R. Buckley wounded. 2/Lt E.C. Mausch wounded. Lt E. Lyed assumed command of the company.	
	17/8/17 18/8/17		6 O.R's killed, 18 wounded, 1 missing. 10 O.R's wounded. 2/Lt 20 = Duncan demobbed being released by the 38th Division. The company in the line were relieved by the 115th M.G. Company. Relief completed at 10 p.m. and company arrived back at camp MALAKOFF FARM AREA at about 3 am 19/8/17.	
	19/8/17		Company left MALAKOFF FARM AREA about 4.30 p.m. passing DAWSON'S CORNER at 4.40 p.m + entraining at ELVERDINGHE at 6 p.m. for the PROVEN AREA. Transport left (by road) at 4.30. The company detrained between INTERNATIONAL CORNER + PROVEN and marched to camp at X 29.C.33 (SALEM CAMP) arriving at 10.30.	
	20/8/17 21/8/17 22/8/17 23/8/17		2/Lieut C. Gray and 2/Lieut H.H.J. Pratt joined Company 2/Lieut V.G. Brereden 2/Lieut R.G. Betts 2/Lieut W.L. Marston 2/Lieut N.L. Turton joined Company. 35 O.R's joined company reinforcements. 19 O.R's " " "	
	24/8/17		10 O.R's (59th Bde) attached to Company. Capt. A.E. Rollings (M.C.) assumed and took command of company. (Suez Camp)	Ref. Sht. 17 1/40
	3/8/17		Lt R.A. Lumb assumed command from BASE DEPOT. May 1918 9th MG. Battery, W.G. awarded Military Medal for gallant conduct under heavy Shell fire at LANGEMARCK on 18/8/17	Appendix 2 showing strength increase + decrease for the month (attached)

[signature]
For Commanding 2nd M.G. Company

20th Divn Operations
Operation Orders No 1.   207 M.G. Coy.

1. Attack is to be in three bounds
   (a) To Blue Line (Front End of LANGEMARCK inclusive of road & houses on each side.) Pause of 20 mins for consolidation
   (b) To Green Line U22 b 8.2 U23 c 6.6.
       U23 d 05 00   U29 b 3.4.
       Pause of 1 hour for consolidation.
   (c) To Red line U17 c 8 2. to U24 c 2 0.
       inclusive of GHELUVELT - LANGEMARCK line.
       Final Objective

2. Sixteen guns of 207 M.G. Coy. will be placed in position on a line about 100x W of the STEENBEEK to place a protective barrage in front of the Green & Red Lines.
    Targets & rates of fire will be as shown on attached table.
    (M.G. Organisation Order No 4.)

3. If possible emplacements will be dug on night 12/13th in shell holes as far as possible will be organised for fire. Guns will be brought into position about 1 hr before Zero. Laying can be done after Zero.

4. The ammunition dumps will be formed on the night 12th/13th close behind the guns. Each section will send parties back with empty belt boxes to be replaced by full boxes as required. All such parties should be formed parties under a N.C.O.

5. After each belt guns should be oiled & pulled through & the laying checked.

6. Sections will be grouped as follows
A section G group
B " H "
C " K "
D " L "

R A Lumby
Comm'g 217 M.G. Coy.

10/8/17

APPENDIX. I.

Dispositions of Machine Guns in Divisional Front.

Forward Positions.

Left Group
1. U 27 d 10.60
2. U 27 d 25.65 Section H.Q.
3. U 27 d 50.60
4. U 27 d 92.56

Right Group
1. U 27 d 90.55 Section H.Q.
2. U 28 c 20.30
3. C 3 b. 20.30
4. C 3 b. 45.30

Rear Positions

Left Group
1. C 2 b. 95.19
2. C 2 b. 92.04
3. C 2 b. 90.55
4. C 2 b. 88.70
   C 2 c 75.30 Section H.Q.

Right Group
1. C 2 d 70.80
2. C 2 d 70.70
3. C 3 c 20.55
4. C 9 a 45.80
   C 27 a 75.05 Section H.Q.
   U. 27 c 75.05 Advanced Coy. Hdqtrs.

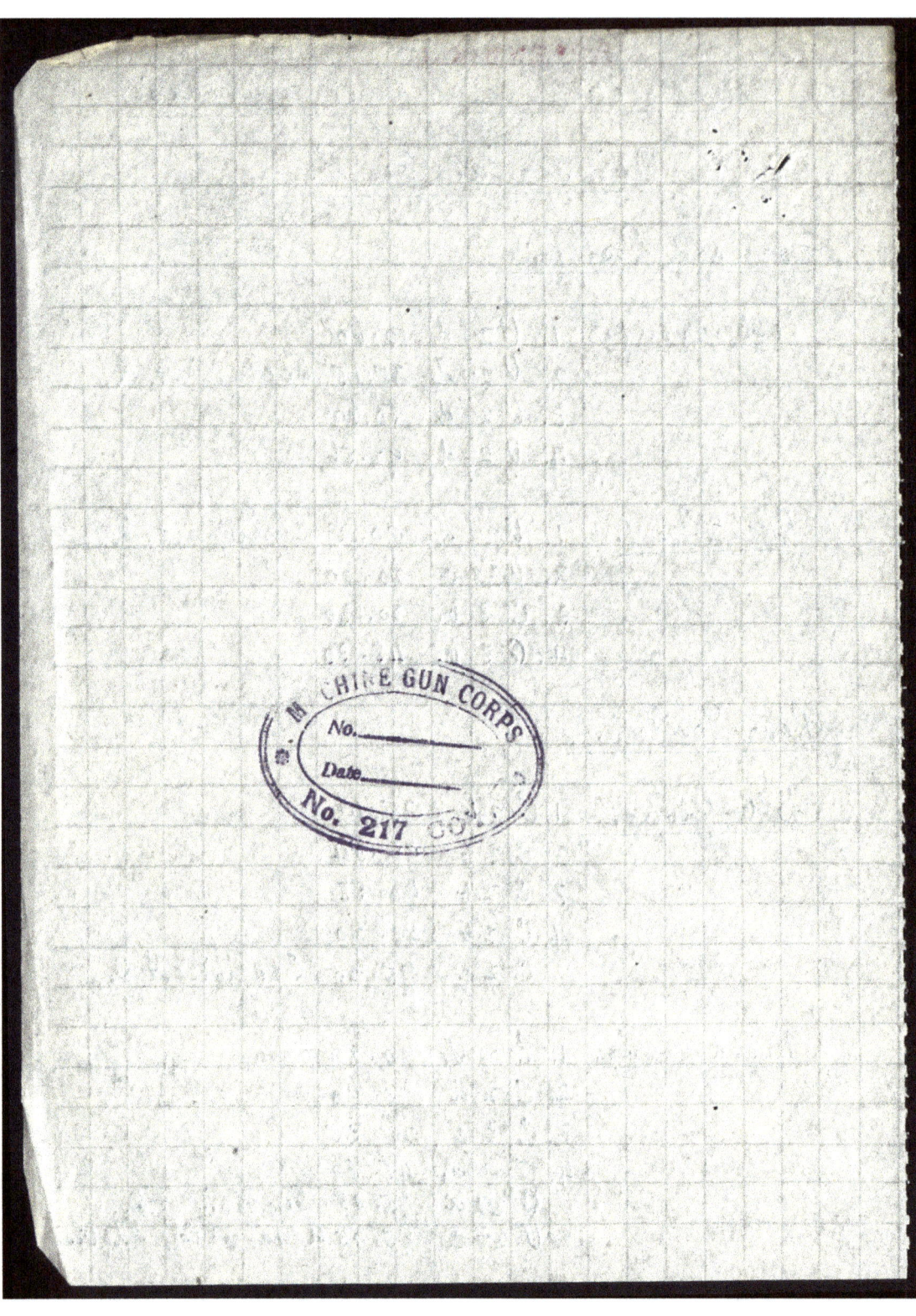

APPENDIX I.

Barrage lines. To be fired when S.O.S. is sent up by infantry.

Forward Groups

Left

	GUN	TARGET	RANGE	Q.E.	MAGNETIC BEARING
1	U27d 1.6	U28b 7.8	1400ˣ	1° 57'	79°
2	U27d 25.65	U28b 8.6	1350ˣ	1° 48'	83°
3	U27d 5.6	U28b 95.40	1350ˣ	1° 48'	86°
4	U27d 92.56	U29a 1.5 to U29a 1.0	1350ˣ	1° 48'	88°

Right

	GUN	TARGET	RANGE	Q.E.	MAGNETIC BEARING
1	U27d 90.55	From U22c 8.4	1400ˣ	1° 57'	37° to 47°
2	U28c 20.30		1400ˣ	1° 57'	32° to 42°
3	U28c 20.30	To U28b 7.8	1400ˣ	1° 57'	37° to 47°
4	C3b 45.30		1750ˣ	2° 35'	52° to 62°

Rear Positions

Left

	GUN	TARGET	RANGE	Q.E.	MAGNETIC BEARING
1	C2b 88.70	From	2100ˣ	4° 32'	67°
2	C2b 90.55	U22c 8.4	2100ˣ	4° 32'	68°
3	C2b 95.19	To	2100ˣ	4° 32'	64°
4	C2b 92.04	U28b 7.8	2100ˣ	4° 32'	72°

Right

	GUN	TARGET	RANGE	Q.E.	MAGNETIC BEARING
1	C2d 7.8	From	2500ˣ	7° 15'	69°
2	C2d 7.7	U28b 7.8	2600ˣ	8° 3'	72°
3	C3c 20.35	To	2600ˣ	8° 3'	66°
4	C9a 45.80	U29a 1.0	2600ˣ	8° 3'	62°

Each gun traverses left to right up to target of next gun.

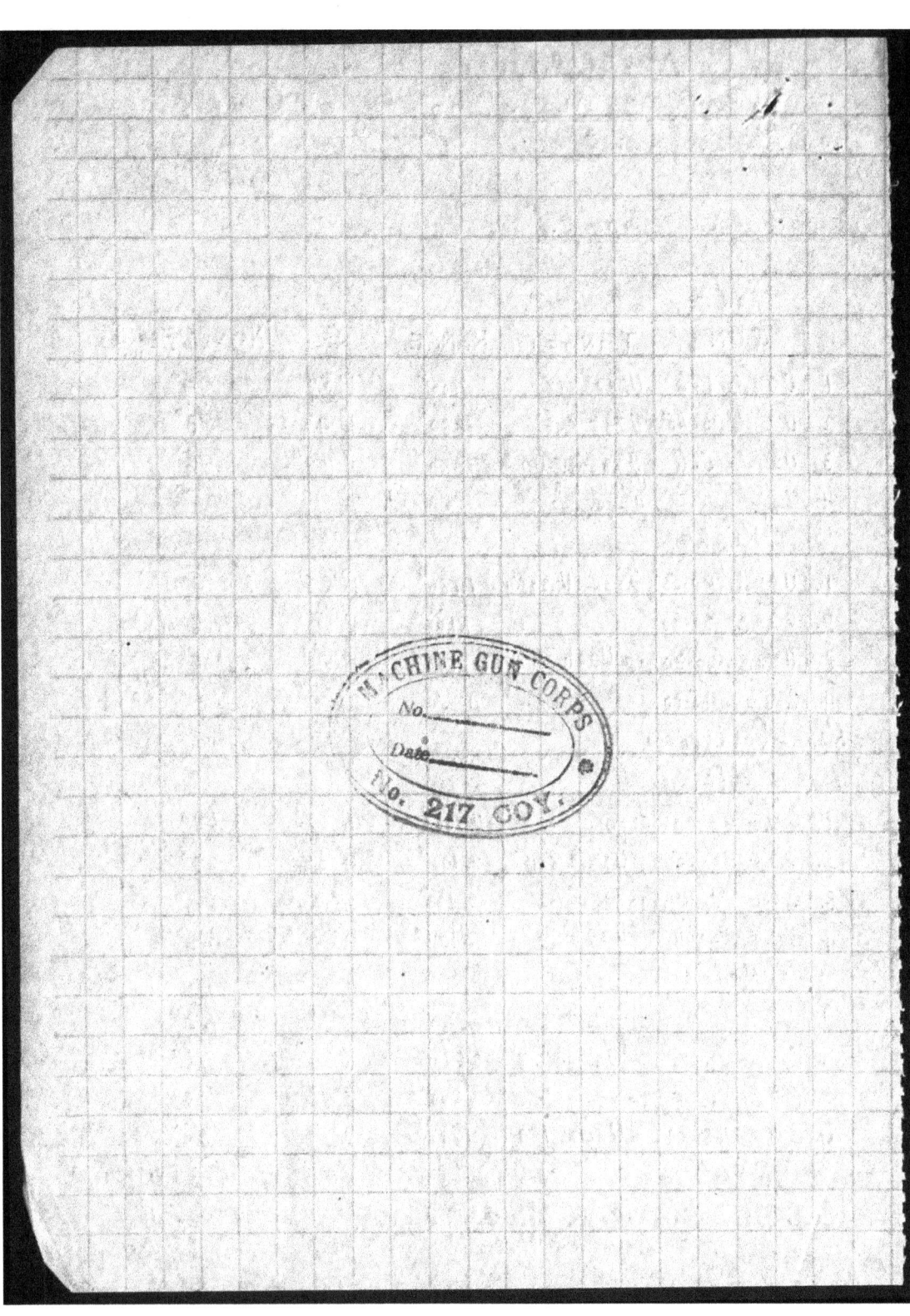

Machine Gun Fire Organisation Order No. 4   217 M.G. Company

No. of Group	No. of Guns	Composition	Commander	Location	Firing from	to	Target	Rate of Fire	Remarks
G	4	One Section of 217 M.G. Coy	2/Lt R. Brierley	About U28c 95.15	1 hour	2.30	g' V30a 21.85 to V23d 99.24	50 rnds per min	S.O.S when called for
					2.30	3.15	g' V24d 70.30 to V24d 01.89	50 rnds per min	S.O.S when called for. Remain laid until further orders.
H	4	One Section of 217 M.G. Coy	2/Lt A.H. Brown	About U28c 87.23	1 hour	2.30	h' V23d 89.26 to V23d 91.77	50 rnds per min	S.O.S when called for.
					2.30	3.15	k' V24d 01.89 to V24a 74.33	50 rnds per min	S.O.S when called for. Remain laid until further orders.
K	4	One Section of 217 M.G. Coy	2/Lt G.S. Hall	About U28c 79.33	1 hour	2.30	k' V23d 91.77 to V23b 64.19	50 rnds per min	S.O.S when called for.
					2.30	3.15	k' V24a 74.33 to V24a 40.75	50 rnds per min	S.O.S when called for. Remain laid until further orders.
L	4	One Section of 217 M.G. Coy	2/Lt E.C. Walsh	About U28c 71.42	1 hour	2.30	L V23b 66.24 to V23b 28.57	50 rnds per min	S.O.S when called for.
					2.30	3.15	L' V24a 40.75 to V18c 10.21	50 rnds per min	S.O.S when called for. Remain laid until further orders.

On "S.O.S" rapid for 1st ten minutes, then 2000 rounds per hour per gun. 2000 rounds in belts must always be kept with each gun to answer "S.O.S" call.

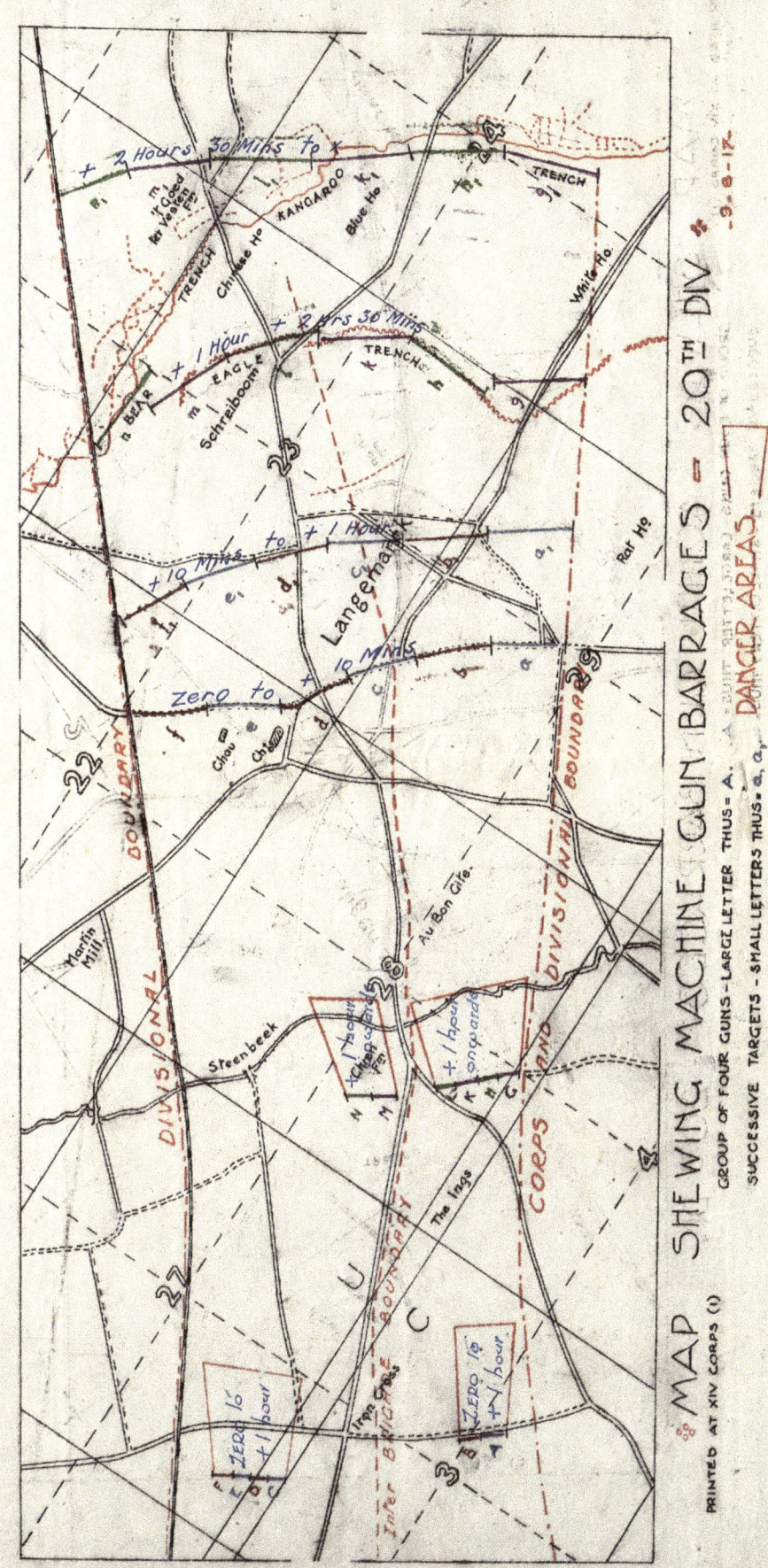

APPENDIX 2.

217 Machine Gun Company

Appendix to War Diary shewing Strength Increase & Decrease for month ending 31.8.17.

Date	No.	Rank	Name	Remarks
2.8.17	19377	Pte.	Edwards J.	Wounded.
3.8.17	45270	L/c	Bland W.	Gassed & Shell Shock
"	19196	Pte.	Roberts W.	Evac. to 63 C.C.S.
4.8.17		2nd Lieut.	T. Johnson	Died of wounds at 46 C.C.S.
"	65196	Pte.	Chilvers H.H.	Rejoined Coy. from C.C.S.
"	7556	Dvr.	Firth E.	" " " 3rd Can. Sty. Hosp.
5.8.17	67742	L/c	Freestone P.M.	Evac. to C.C.S.
"	20196	"	Laird A.	
6.8.17	19377	Pte.	Edwards J.	Rejd. Coy. (previously reported wounded)
"		T/2nd Lieut.	A.R. Mettam	Joined Coy.
7.8.17	72160	Pte.	Williams E.	Leave to U.K. 8.8.17 – 18.8.17
9.8.17	35199	Cpl.	Reynolds J.W.	Rejd. Coy. from Course.
10.8.17		Lieut.	E.L. Yeo	Rejd. Coy. from Course.
"	64080	Pte.	Wilmore R.	" " " " (Batman)
"	16035	"	Wallington H.	Leave to U.K. 11.8.17 – 21.8.17
"	43078	"	Burden G.	Killed in action.
"	200319	Rfn.	Wood W. (10th R.B. attached)	Evac. to C.C.S.
11.8.17	3196	L/c	Barker J.	" " " "
13.8.17	10355	Pte.	Mowbray J.W.	Rejd. Coy. off leave to U.K.
14.8.17	10011	"	Ashcroft H.	Killed in action.
"	34379	Rfn.	Smith H.W. (10th K.R.R.C. attached)	Killed in action.
"	4595	Pte.	Wood J.	Wounded.
"	19813	"	Hoskins B.	do.
"	20048	Cpl.	Walker J.	do.
"	6017	C.S.M.	Gannon J.	Leave to U.K. 15.8.17 – 25.8.17
"	85767	Sgt	Dow-Smith G.	Transferred to 46th M.G. Coy.
15.8.17	5041	L/c	Sealey J.	
"	31055	Pte.	Cowie J.	Reported missing.
"	19796	Rfn.	Phillips (10th R.B. attached)	
16.8.17		T/2nd Lieut.	A.R. Mettam	
"	36049	Pte.	Beade D.	
"	65208	"	Cockerill A.J.	
"	3776	L/c	Cockings E.	Killed in action.
"	66651	Pte.	Bloodworth H.	
"	200225	Rfn.	Pickett W. (10th K.R.R.C. attached)	
"	22846	"	Taylor J.C. (11th K.R.R.C. attached)	
"		Lieut.	R.A. Lumb	
"		2/Lieut.	R. Buckley	
"		"	G.S. Ball	
"		"	C.C. Walsch	
"	17772	Sgt.	Wright R.	Wounded.
"	22639	"	Hextall C.J.	
"	24561	Cpl.	Leitch J.W.	
"	42773	L/c	Simpson C.	
"	42647	Pte.	McKenzie C.	
"	26336	"	Kingsley E.	

SHEET II.

Date.	No.	Rk.	Name	Remarks.
16.8.17	7191	Pte.	Clipstone G.	
✓	67727	✓	Crawford A.S.	
✓	57765	✓	Jackson W.	
✓	67721	✓	Hornaby S.	
✓	58313	✓	Davidson A.	
✓	67732	✓	Ball W.	Wounded.
✓	19377	✓	Edwards J.	
✓	30058	✓	Blundell G.	
✓	81896	✓	Cook G.A.	
✓	67741	✓	Cull A.J.	
✓	20376	L/c	Cluness A.J.	
✓	38295	Rfn	Dean S. (10th K.R.R.C attached)	missing.
✓	28157	✓	Lock J.G. (10th R.B attached)	
✓	64853	Dvr.	Hamer R.	Evac. to C.C.S.
✓	43460	Pte.	Evans G.	Killed in Action
17.8.17	67722	L/c	Hornaby E.W.	Evac. to C.C.S.
✓	67799	Pte.	Goddard A.	Rejd. from C.C.S.
18.8.17	19196	✓	Roberts W.	Died of wounds at 18 C.M.D.S.
✓	64080	✓	Wilmore R.	
19.8.17	2/Lieut.		G. Gay	Joined Coy.
✓		✓	H.H.J. Pratt	
✓	2/Lieut.		W.J. Hutton	Rejoined Coy. from Course.
✓	7147	Sgt	Simpson W.B. (Batman)	
✓	6250	Pte.	Smith G.	Rejd. Coy. off leave to U.K.
20.8.19	72169	✓	Williams E.	Rejoined Coy.
✓	19813	✓	Hoskins B.	Evac. to C.C.S
✓	63661	Dvr.	Morley J.	
✓	2/Lieut.		W.L.J. Walton	
✓		✓	H.L. Turton	Joined Coy.
✓		✓	R.G. Betts	
✓		✓	V.G.C. Breeden	
21.8.17	19873	Sgt	Buttery W.J.	Leave to U.K. 25.8.17 – 1.9.17
✓	32025	Rfn	Chance R. (11th K.R.R.C. attached)	Evac. to C.C.S.
22.8.17	16035	Pte.	Wallington H.	Rejd. Coy. off leave to U.K.
✓	55927	L/c	Chadwell M.C.	
✓	30901	Pte.	Ansell S.	
✓	67723	✓	Gallagher S.	Joined Coy. from XIV. Corps Rest Camp BOLLEZEELE.
✓	105967	✓	Cresswell L.	
✓	102971	✓	Drummond H.A.	
✓	89433	✓	Dunn S.B.	
✓	88363	✓	Dunn R.	

SHEET III.

Date	No.	Rk	Name	Remarks
22.8.17	102341	Pte.	Freeman S.	
✓	106061	✓	Forrester J.	
✓	99989	✓	Goodwille J.	
✓	104110	✓	Johnson G.	
✓	36717	✓	Jones W.L.	
✓	103107	✓	Kerr R.	
✓	106066	✓	Kerr W.	
✓	18478	✓	Law H.	
✓	103122	✓	Lambert F.	
✓	106056	✓	Lees J.	
✓	106033	✓	Murdoch D.	
✓	103898	✓	Murr G.A.	
✓	106063	✓	Macara C.W.	Joined Coy. from XIV.
✓	106091	✓	McNey J.J.	Corps Rest Camp
✓	103902	✓	Brewitt A.	BOLLEZEELE.
✓	86101	✓	Budden F.A.	
✓	89130	✓	Ramsay A.H.	
✓	81588	✓	Rosbrook C.W.	
✓	37993	✓	Scott S.	
✓	106340	✓	Shaw G.	
✓	106093	✓	Stuart W.	
✓	24506	✓	Städig J.H.	
✓	106245	✓	Terry F.D.	
✓	103949	✓	Thurkle W.H.	
✓	51124	✓	Weare E.	
✓	104922	✓	Weir J.	
✓	26391	✓	Young J.	
✓	106350	✓	Youngs S.A.	
23.8.17		2/Lieut	W. Lee Wilson	Rejd. Coy. off Leave to U.K.
✓	8848	Pte.	Shackleton J.	Evac. to C.C.S.
✓	7877	Dvr.	Webb G.	✓ ✓ ✓
✓	3253	L/c	Mullins R.J.	
✓	5948	Pte.	Cartmell J.	
✓	20712	✓	Ford J.H.	
✓	44792	✓	Judge W.	Joined Coy. from BASE
✓	103112	✓	Goldstraw R.	DEPOT.
✓	53159	✓	Hadwick A.	
✓	104366	✓	May J.	
✓	90186	✓	Hathan J.	
✓	25803	✓	Brook S.	
✓	103634	✓	Smith W.H.	

SHEET IV.

Date.	No.	Rk.	Name	Remarks
23.8.17	6476	Pte.	Southworth J.	
✓	3626	✓	Sutton C.	
✓	73756	✓	Shaw E. A.	
✓	7953	✓	Slack F. O.	
✓	68211	✓	Volckman J.	Joined Coy. from BASE DEPOT.
✓	10248	✓	Wallwork J.	
✓	87097	✓	Weston C.	
✓	43111	✓	Weston R.	
✓	64635	✓	Sonton E. F.	
24.8.17	Capt.		A. E. Rollings M.C.	Joined Coy.
✓	8125	Rfn	Cripps G. (10th R.B attached)	
✓	200986	✓	Brown F. (do)	
✓	37357	✓	Hinham G. (10th K.R.R attached)	
✓	36741	✓	Keen A. (do)	
✓	31947	✓	Wickman H. (do)	Joined Coy. from respective Units.
✓	32141	✓	Jacques F. (11th K.R.R attached)	
✓	307	✓	Palmer J. (do)	
✓	2143	✓	Allsopp G. (do)	
✓	13110	✓	Douglas J. (11th R.B. attached)	
✓	203568	✓	Hayman H. (do)	
25.8.17	20259	Cpl	Brooker F. E.	Rejd. Coy. from Course.
26.8.17	200319	Rfn.	Wood W. (10th R.B attached)	Rejd Coy. from C.C.S.
27.8.17		Capt.	A. E. Rollings M.C.	Leave to U.K. 29.8.17 to 7.9.17
28.8.17	20752	a/Sgt.	Barker G. F.	Leave to U.K 29.8.17 - 29.9.17
✓	50980	Pte.	Wilson A.	
✓	105519	✓	Taylor F.	
✓	52639	✓	Druitt H.	
✓	52596	✓	Woods W.	
✓	52162	✓	Jones E.	
✓	52287	✓	Rosser J. A.	
✓	47016	✓	Jerkins J. W.	Joined Coy. from BASE DEPOT.
✓	52618	✓	Lea R.	
✓	52696	✓	Brett C.	
✓	105514	✓	Curran J.	
✓	52136	✓	Rogers F. J.	
✓	52804	✓	Inckrose C.	
✓	105208	✓	Hogg J.	
✓	105350	✓	Silverwood L.	
✓	50775	✓	Dobbs J.	
✓	52385	✓	Collett A. R.	
✓	105515	✓	Smith C.	
✓	105440	✓	Coffey W.	

SHEET V

Date	No.	Rk.	Name	Remarks
28.8.17	105319	Pte.	Eason R.	
✓	47361	✓	McGarry J.	
✓	52357	✓	Hunter J.	
✓	51891	✓	Keay E.	
✓	52568	✓	Selley J.	
✓	105422	✓	Day W.J.	
✓	52661	✓	Daniels A.	
✓	47574	✓	Ellis G.H.	
✓	47376	✓	Gordon B.B.	Joined Coy. from BASE DEPOT.
✓	105383	✓	Hutchinson C.F.	
✓	105368	✓	Olley M.C.	
✓	105425	✓	McKennan A.G.	
✓	105490	✓	Paterson J.	
✓	105391	✓	Gott J.	
✓	105357	✓	Sower A.	
✓	65012	✓	Mitchell J.	
✓	47016	✓	Fairhall J.	
30.8.17	21583	A/Sgt.	Lamb W.	To Course
✓	28741	Rfn.	Heyden A.G. (11th RB attached)	Rej'd. Coy. from Unit.
✓		Lieut.	R.A. Lumb	Joined Coy. from BASE DEPOT.
Honours + Awards.				
31.8.17	19873	Sgt.	Buttery W.G.	Awarded Military Medal Authority XIV Corps No 2583/2609 dated 30/8/17.

Vol 7

WAR DIARY

217 Machine Gun
Coy — Sept 1917

Army Form C. 2118.

WAR DIARY
or
INTELLIGENCE SUMMARY.
(Erase heading not required.)

Instructions regarding War Diaries and Intelligence Summaries are contained in F. S. Regs., Part II and the Staff Manual respectively. Title pages will be prepared in manuscript.

No. 1

Place	Date	Hour	Summary of Events and Information	Remarks and references to Appendices
PROVEN AREA (St. CAMPS) SUEZ CAMP	1/9/17		Company at rest at SUEZ CAMP x 19 d.1.3. No. 10317 4/Cpl CLUNESS.A.T. awarded Military Medal for gallantry whilst engaged in the operations near LANGEMARCK on 16/8/17.	Sheet 19. 1/40000
	5/9/17	9 a.m	Presentation of medal ribbon by Divisional Commander.	
	9/9/17	7.30 p.m	These Gun teams of 'A' Section relieved 3 gun teams of 113th M.G. Coy. for Anti Aircraft duty at JOLIE FARM. C9a.3.6. The Division commenced relieving the 38th (Welsh) Division in the line, finishing relief on 11/9/17.	Sheet 28 N.W. 1/20000
	10/9/17	11 a.m	The Company moved to the MALAKOFF FARM AREA. B22 & 8% entraining at INTERNATIONAL CORNER & detraining at ELVERDINGHE. Transport proceeded by road to the Company Transport lines at B23 a 3.6. in the CANADA FARM AREA. 'B' Section relieved 'A' Section at the Anti Aircraft position (JOLIE FARM) leaving camp at 3.30 a.m.	
	13/9/17		'D' Section left camp at 3.30 a.m to perform barrage position in the line. The Company (less 'B' Section) left camp at 6 P.M. to take over barrage positions in the line from the 50th M.G. Coy.	Rd. RELIEF PAPER No. 1 (attached) see Appendix M.4 for Organization
	15/9/17			
	18/9/17		On the night of 18/9/17 unit the '61st' Infy Bde was relieved in the line by the 60th Infy Bde. The 61st Infy Bde in the left Divisional sector in the night. Divisional Sector + the 50th Infy Bde in the left Divisional Sector.	Order with Divisional M.G.C.

WAR DIARY
INTELLIGENCE SUMMARY

Army Form C. 2118.

Instructions regarding War Diaries and Intelligence Summaries are contained in F.S. Regs., Part II. and the Staff Manual respectively. Title pages will be prepared in manuscript.

(Erase heading not required.)

Place	Date	Hour	Summary of Events and Information	Remarks and references to Appendices
	20/9/17		The XIV. Corps attack was carried out by the 1st. Division simultaneously with the XVIII Corps (61st Division) on the right. The Guards Division on the left were not engaged in their operation.	Sheet 28 N.W.
			The camp at MALAKOFF FARM AREA B.21.b.8.5 shelled about 5:30 p.m. with H.V. shells and compelled the company details left out of battle to move down to BRIDGE JUNCTION B.20.b.3.7 together with the transport lines. 1 O.R. was killed + 1 O.R. wounded in the line. Also 1 O.R. killed + 1 O.R. wounded in the line.	German Aeroplane down
	21/9/17		1 O.R. killed. 1 O.R. wounded. 1 O.R. shell shock.	
	22/9/17		2 O.Rs killed. 2 O.Rs wounded.	
	23/9/17		The 61st Inf. Bde. took over the Divisional front. 1 O.R. wounded.	Rd. LANGEMARCK
	24/9/17		On the night of 23/24 the following moves took place :- (a) 1 section from Railway Junction to reserve at Advance Company H.Q. C.4.a.75.75. (b) 3 Sections from Railway Junction to Front Line relieving section of 59th + 60th M.G. Coys. 1 O.R. wounded.	
	25/9/17		The 21st Divison commenced heavy bombardment in the line by the 4 H.E. + 2 gas Livens Projectors.	
	26/9/17		On the night to effect the confusion was relieved in the line by 3 sections of 185 M.G. Coy and 1 section of 28 M.G. Coy. Our bombardment by Livens Projectors (at BRIDGE JUNCTION) about midnight	
	27/9/17			

Army Form C. 2118.

WAR DIARY
or
INTELLIGENCE SUMMARY.
(Erase heading not required.)

Instructions regarding War Diaries and Intelligence Summaries are contained in F. S. Regs., Part II. and the Staff Manual respectively. Title pages will be prepared in manuscript.

Place	Date	Hour	Summary of Events and Information	Remarks and references to Appendices
	28/9/17		Company left camp at BRIDGE JUNCTION at 3.30 P.M for the PROVEN AREA (St Cambier). Transport left by road + remainder entrained at ELVERDINGHE at 4.15 P.M. On arrival in this area the company remained encamped at STAFFORD CAMP F6a.1.5 for the remainder of the month.	Sheet 28 1/40000

[signature] Lieut.
for Commanding 217 M.G. Company

[stamp: MACHINE GUN CORPS No. 217]

APPENDIX 2.
Casualty Report
for month ending Sept. 29th 1917

217 M.G. Coy.   "In the Field"

Month	Day	Remarks
Sept 1917	1	52357 Pte. Hunter J. 65256 " Wilbourne G. 66650 " Lee W. 20358 Rfn. Hayman H. (11th R.B) attached) } Admitted to Hospital 3625 Pte. Sutton J. rejoined Coy. from Hospital.
	2	65203 Pte. Bell D.G. proceeded to Rest Camp at EQUIHEM. 66413 Pte. Morbey A. rejoined Coy. from Hospital. 203568 Rfn. Hayman H. (11th R.B) Evacuated to C.C.S.
	3	55368 Pte. Vaughan A.E. (To C.C.S.) 28070 Rfn. Young G. (11th R.B) attached } Admitted to Hospital. 19873 Sgt. Buttery W.G. rejoined Coy. off leave to U.K.
	4	104366 Pte. May J. admitted to Hospital Lieut. E.L. Yeo proceeded on leave to U.K.
	5	3625 Pte. Sutton J. admitted to Hospital 65256 Pte. Wilbourne G. } Rejoined Coy. from Hospital 89539 " Ramsay A.H. 12794 Dvr. Palmer A. proceeded on leave to U.K. 52357 Pte. Hunter J. Evacuated to C.C.S.
	6	36717 Pte. Jones W.L. admitted to Hospital & evacuated to C.C.S.
	7	6138 Dvr. Blackwell E. 106056 Pte. Lees J. (To C.C.S.) } Admitted to Hospital. 16684 Pte. Harris A.S. } Rejoined Coy. from Hospital. 3625 " Sutton J. 2/Lieut. N.L. Turton admitted to XIV Corps Rest Stn. 12586 Pte. O'Callaghan J. proceeded on Cookery Course.
	8	16684 Pte. Harris A.S. } admitted to Hospital. 3625 " Sutton J. 2/Lieut. N.L. Turton } Evacuated to C.C.S. 200210 Rfn. Percival J. 28070 Rfn. Young G. rejoined Coy. from Hospital.
	10	66650 Pte. Lee W. rejoined Coy. from Hospital.

SHEET II

Month	Day	Remarks
Sept 1917	11	25803 L/c. Brooke S. 105908 Pte. Hogg J. 37357 Rfn. Ninham (10 K.R.R.C.) attached } admitted to Hospital 22630 Sgt. Hextall C.J. joined Coy. from Base Depot. 45261 Pte. Heighington J. 60304 " Rooth C. } Proceeded on Leave to U.K.
	12	52661 Pte. Daniels A. admitted to Hospital.
	13	2/Lieut. D Knox Brown M.C. 43922 Sgt. Moore J. 72169 Pte. Williams E. } Proceeded on Infantry Course. 38298 Rfn. Thomas A admitted to Hospital.
	14	50980 Pte. Wilson A.W. admitted to Hospital.
	16	68224 Pte. Voeckman H proceeded on course of Sanitation. 17817 Rfn. Cohen J. (11th R.B.) attached, admitted to Hosp. 17000 Cpl. Pulford W.C. 67801 Pte. Tyler H } Proceeded to Rest Camp at EQUIHEM.
	17	105383 Pte. Hutchinson C proceeded on Leave to U.K. Lieut. E.L. Yeo 12794 Dvr. Palmer A } Rejoined Coy. off Leave to U.K. 103634 Pte. Smith W.H. 200319 Rfn. Wood W } Admitted to Hospital.
	18	6138 Dvr. Blackwell E. rejoined Coy. from Hospital. 63652 Dvr. Newton F. admitted to Hospital. 105514 L/c. Curran J. 46524 " Davies E. } Proceeded on Leave to U.K.
	19	36521 Rfn. Beard J (10 K.R.R.C.) attached admitted to Hosp. 16684 Pte. Harris A.S. 3625 " Sutton J. 105208 " Hogg J. } Evacuated to C.C.S. 106066 Pte. Kerr W. wounded. 12586 Pte O'Callaghan J rejoined Coy. from Cookery Course.

SHEET III

Month	Day	Remarks
Sept 1917	20	Capt A.E. Rollings M.C. rejoined Coy off leave to U.K.
		12586 Pte. O'Callaghan J. proceeded on leave to U.K.
		50980 Pte. Wilson A.W. rejoined Coy. from Hospital.
		103634 Pte. Smith W.A. ⎫
		37357 Rfn. Kinham J. (10th K.R.R.C) attached ⎬ Evacuated
		200319 " Wood W. (10 R.B.) do. ⎭ to C.C.S.
		55927 L/C. Chadwell M.C. Killed in action.
		21022 Rfn. Meade H. (11th R.B.) attached. Killed.
		65203 Pte. Bell D.G. Wounded.
		65196 " Chelvers J. do.
	21	200287 Rfn. Harrison G. (10 R.B.) attached Killed in Action.
		47435 Pte. Perkins T.W. Wounded
		106065 " Macara C.W. Buried.
		52385 L/C. Collett A.G. do.
		89530 Pte. Ramsay A.H. Shell Shock
	22	105390 Pte. Paterson C. Wounded.
		24558 Cpl. Greig J. ⎫ admitted to Hospital.
		3532 L/C. Bane E. ⎭
		19196 L/C Roberts W. ⎫ Killed in Action.
		83600 Pte. Lualo G.J. ⎭
		105440 Pte. Coffey W. Wounded.
	23	103125 L/C. Lambert J. do.
		68221 Pte. Volckman rejoined Coy. from Course of Sanitation.
	24	30044 L/C Smith A. admitted to Hospital
		45261 Pte. Heighington G. ⎫ Rejoined Coy off Leave to U.K.
		60304 " Booth C. ⎭
		52661 Pte. Daniels A. rejoined Coy. from Hospital.
		20259 Sgt. Brooker J.E. Wounded
	26	60390 C.Q.M.S Walker W.J. ⎫ Proceeded on Leave to U.K.
		24212 Dvr. Hogg G. ⎭
	27	53159 Pte. Hadwick A. ⎫ admitted to Hospital.
		51891 " Keay E. ⎭
		17817 Rfn. Cohen J. (11th R.B.) attached ⎫ Rejd. from
		36717 Pte. Jones W.L. ⎭ Hospital.
		106033 Pte. Murdoch D. Killed in Action.
		104950 " Weir J. Wounded.
		2/Lt. W.S Hutton proceeded on Leave to U.K.

SHEET IV.

No. 217 COY.

Month	Day	Remarks
1917 Sept.	28	37159 Pte. Drye R.C. } Proceeded to Rest Camp at 6250 " Smith G. } EQUIHEM. 17009 Cpl. Pulford W.C. } Rejoined Coy. from Rest Camp 67801 Pte. Tyler H } at EQUIHEM. 52618 Pte. Lea R. proceeded on Leave to U.K. 25803 L/c. Brooke S. rejoined Coy. from Hospital.
	29	24558 Cpl. Greig J. rejoined Coy. from Hospital. 21583 a/Sgt. Lamb W. rejoined Coy. from Course at small arms School CAMIERS. 50908 Pte. Wilson A.W. admitted to Hospital 28377 Pte. Munro H. 107376 " Dorrell J. 49117 " Payne A.G. 104911 " Brotheridge H.W. } Joined Coy. from Base Depot. 67805 " Thompson C.J. 72029 " Tyson R.C. 43556 " Burgess H.E. 105383 Pte. Hutchinson C. rejd. Coy. off Leave to U.K.
	30	11636 Signaller Freeman A.M. 2143 Rfm. Allsopp G. (11 R.B.) attached } Admitted to Hospital. 57646 Pte. Woodcock L. 105514 L/c. Curran J. } Rejd. Coy. off Leave to U.K. 46527 " Davies E. Lieut. R.A. Lumb 55927 Sgt. Gritto G.H. } Proceeded on Course to Small 10,524 Pte. Barnett S. } Arms School CAMIERS.

SECRET   COPY No 6

Ref BIXSCHOOTE 1/10,000

Relief Orders - 217 Machine Gun Coy

1. The 217 M.G. Coy will take over approximate barrage positions at present occupied by 59 M.G. Coy on the night of the 17th Sept 1917.

2. The Coy less B Section will move up from MALAKOFF FARM area at 6pm to CANAL BANK. Limbers will proceed via BRIELEN and ESSEX FARM, and personnel via duckboard track to Bridge 6 - about 400x S of BARD'S CAUSEWAY. Limbers will be unloaded here & equipment & guns loaded on light railway trucks. If night is favourable trucks may be taken to AU BON GITE but otherwise guns &c will be unloaded where railway crosses road at U28.C.65.00

3. Gun positions will be occupied according to letters shewn on BIXSCHOOTE Map, a, b, c, d.

4. When carrying has been completed three men per gun team only will remain at gun positions. Three men will be either in reserve dugout at C4.a.7.7 now occupied by 59th M.G. Coy or in one of positions at present occupied by A.A. Guns.

5. Eight extra belts per gun will be carried in S.A.A. boxes.

6. HQ of A, B & C Sections will be at U.28.6.6.0. in dugout at present occupied by 59th M.G. Coy. Coy HQ and H.Q of D Section will be in dug out near reserve team dug out.

- 2 -

7. Coy HQ will be connected by telephone with Section H.Q.: line will be laid by Coy Signallers at dawn following night of relief.

8. "Relief complete" will be reported to Coy. H.Q by Section Officers either personally or in writing.

9. 2/Lieut R.G. BETTS will remain at camp in MALAKOFF FARM. 2/Lieut H.H.J. PRATT will be in charge of personnel staying at A.A. gun position.

10. If it is impossible to lay a correct aim on aiming posts on relief, guns of 59 M.G. Coy will remain in position until dawn.

11. Guns of A & C Sections will not be mounted, as no guns of 59 M.G. Coy are in these positions.

12. An interval of 500x will be kept between sections.

(sgd) R.A. Lumb Lieut
for Commdg 217 M.G. Coy

COPY No 1   O.C. "A" Section
         2   " "B"
         3   " "C"
         4   " "D"
         5   " Transport
         6   War Diary.

16.9.1917.

SECRET   COPY No 4

Relief Order No II - 217 Machine Gun Coy.

On the night of Sept 27th/28th the Company will be relieved by 12 Guns of 12 M.G. Coy and 4 Guns of 86 M.G. Coy.

6 Guns of 12 M.G. Coy will relieve the 6 Guns commanded by 2/Lieuts BREEDEN and BETTS.

2 Guns of 12 M.G. Coy will relieve the 2 Guns commanded by 2/Lieut WALTON.

4 Guns of 86 M.G. Coy will relieve the 4 Guns commanded by 2/Lieut GAY.

Guides from Coy H.Q. will conduct the relieving teams to the Section H.Q.

Section Officers will arrange for Guides from their respective Gun Teams to be at their H.Q. at 8pm. These Guides will conduct the relieving gun teams to their positions. Reliable Guides must be provided.

Tripods & Belt boxes will be handed over, and receipts taken for same.

Section Officers to explain to the relieving Officers fields of fire & all information regarding their frontage.

On completion of relief Officers will conduct their Sections out of the line & report to Coy H.Q. (ADV) "relief complete".

Guns &c will be dumped at the junction of BARDS CAUSEWAY & the road

- 2 -

where 4 men have been detailed to take charge of them until Limber arrives.

Every endeavour will be made to take the men to Transport Lines in Limbers or Lorries.

ACKNOWLEDGE.

M Yeo Lt
for. Commdg. 217 M.G. Coy.

Copy. No 1   Lieut R.A. LUMB.
 "   No 2   2/Lieuts WALTON & GAY.
 "   No 3   "   BREEDEN & BETTS.
 "   No 4   War Diary.

26.9.1917.

Machine Gun Fire Organization Order   No. 217 M.G. Coy.

No. of Gun in Rty.	No. of Guns	Composition	Commander	Location	Firing from to	Target	Rate of fire	Remarks
A.	4 Guns	"A" Section	2/Lt. W.C.J. Bowles	U.29.c.08.75 (About)	Zero to +2 hrs	V.19.a.25.26 to V.19.a.01.49	One belt in five minutes	After +2 hours these guns will stand fast to answer "S.O.S." calls.
B.	4 Guns	"B" Section	2/Lt. G. Gay	U.28.b.95.04 (About)	Zero to +2 hrs	V.19.a.01.49 to U.24.b.72.75		
C.	4 Guns	"C" Section	2/Lt. N.G. C. Bracken	U.28.d.92.59 (About)	Zero to +2 hrs	U.24.b.72.75 to U.18.d.43.01		
D.	4 Guns	"D" Section	2/Lt. W. Hutton	U.28.d.80.77 (About)	Zero to +2 hrs	U.18.d.43.01 to U.18.d.12.29		

x = rounds per hour per gun.
On "S.O.S." rapid for 1st ten minutes; then 2000 rounds per hour per gun.
2000 rounds in belts must always be kept with each gun to answer "S.O.S." calls.

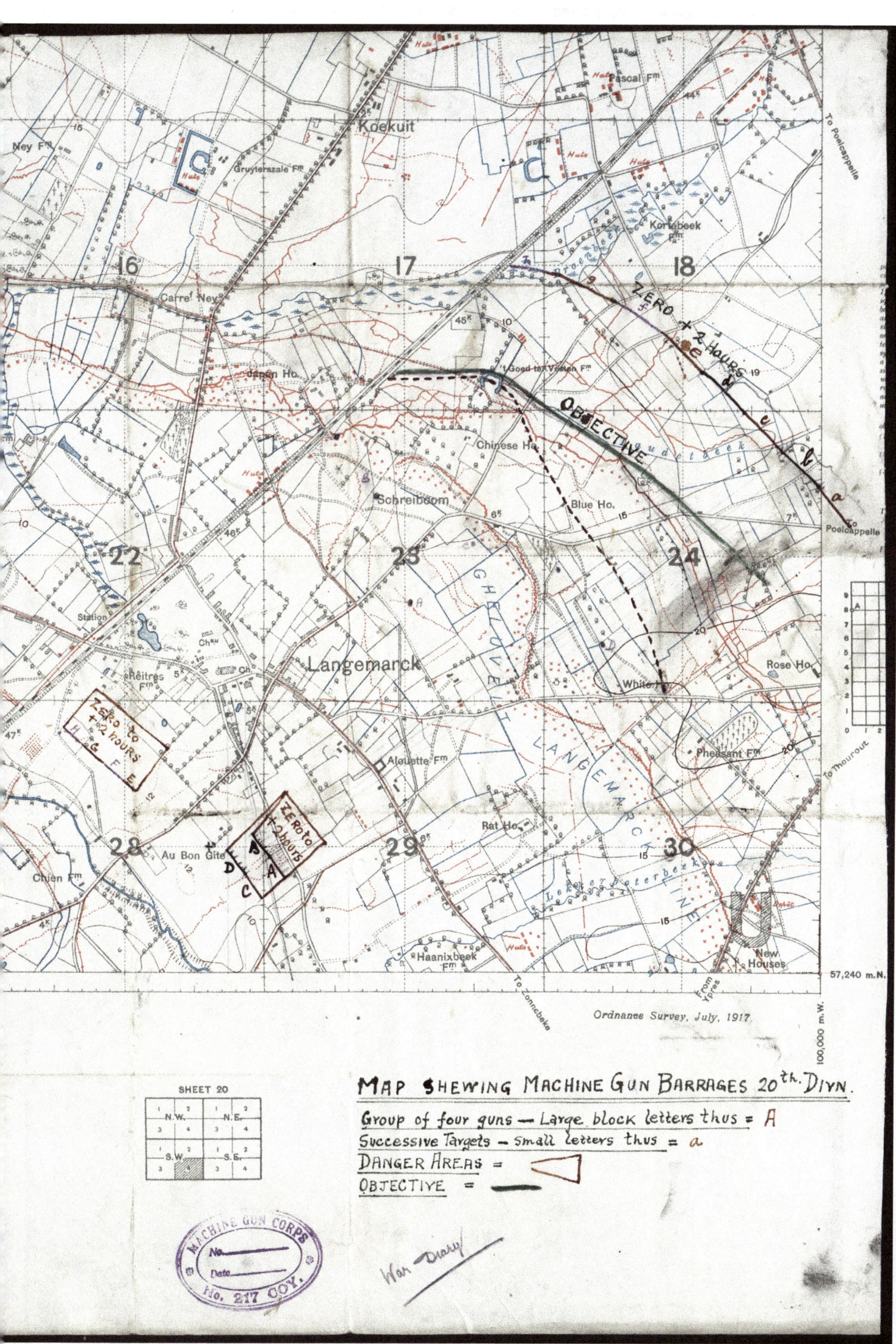

217 M.G. Coy
Army Form C. 2118.

217 M.G. Coy
October 1917.
J.M.S.

WAR DIARY
INTELLIGENCE SUMMARY

Place	Date	Hour	Summary of Events and Information	Remarks and references to Appendices
STAFFORD CAMP.	1	6 a.m.	Advanced Party under 2/Lt. W.R.P. Walton left to take over billets at YTRES.	
STAFFORD CAMP.	2	7 a.m.	Company left STAFFORD CAMP & entrained at HOPOUTRE SIDING. Detained at BAPAUME and proceeded by light railway to billets at YTRES. Arrived 9 p.m.	
YTRES.	3	7 p.m.	One Section of Company ordered to proceed overseas Frontier with M.E.F.: A Section warned.	
YTRES.	4	—	Ordinary Company routine.	
YTRES.	5	—	A Section equipped according to Mob: Table.	
YTRES.	6	9 a.m.	Company proceeded to FINS. 5th area W.13.b. & encamped at SOREL.	
SOREL.	7	—	A Section proceeded overseas. Section Officer Lieut: E.L. YEO. Sub: Sec: Officer V.G.C. BREEDEN.	

Army Form C. 2118.

WAR DIARY
INTELLIGENCE SUMMARY.
(Erase heading not required.)

Instructions regarding War Diaries and Intelligence Summaries are contained in F. S. Regs., Part II. and the Staff Manual respectively. Title pages will be prepared in manuscript.

Place	Date	Hour	Summary of Events and Information	Remarks and references to Appendices
SOREL	8	-		
"	9	-	Ordinary Company routine.	
"	10	-		
"	11.	2.30pm	Company proceeded to billets at HEUDICOURT. Shed 57c. h/20.k.8.6.	
			O.C. Company reconnoitred centre of Divisional front with D.M.G.O. & returned in the afternoon.	
HEUDICOURT.	12	-	Ordinary Company routine.	
"	13	-	2/Lt. R.G. Botts reconnoitred centre of Divisional front returned in the afternoon.	
"	14	-	O.C. Company reconnoitred left of Divisional front & returned in the afternoon.	
"	15	-	2/Lt. G. Gay & 2/Lt. H.H.J. Prall reconnoitred centre of Divisional front & returned in the afternoon.	
"	16	-	2/Lt. N.S. Hutton & 2/Lt. h.R.P. Walton reconnoitred left of Divisional front & returned in the evening.	
"	17/18/19/20	-	Ordinary Company routine.	

Army Form C. 2118.

WAR DIARY
or
INTELLIGENCE SUMMARY.
(Erase heading not required.)

Instructions regarding War Diaries and Intelligence Summaries are contained in F. S. Regs., Part II. and the Staff Manual respectively. Title pages will be prepared in manuscript.

Place	Date	Hour	Summary of Events and Information	Remarks and references to Appendices
HEUDICOURT.	21.	9.30am	Church parade.	
"	22. 23. 24. 25. 26.	-	Ordinary Company routine.	
"	27.	11am	Company inspected by Divisional General [Sir Douglas Smith. C.B.].	
"	28.	9am	Capt. O.E. Rollings proceeded to the 60th Machine Gun Company's H.Q. in the line to make arrangements for relief.	
"	29.	9am	Company relieved 60th M.G. Coy in the line on fall of Divisional front. Relief completed by 2 p.m. new emplacements & shelters dug during the night 29-30 Oct.	
	30.	-	Trench routine.	
	31.	10am	Capt. A.E. Rollings M.C. attended Divisional Conference. S.O.S. & Tactical positions discussed + determined. Defensive Scheme completed.	

W. J. Hutton 2/Lt
O.C. 217 M.G. Coy

Vol 9

24th Trmtho
20th Div

WAR DIARY
217th Machine Gun Coy
NOVEMBER

Army Form C. 2118.

WAR DIARY
INTELLIGENCE SUMMARY.
(Erase heading not required.)

December 1917

Instructions regarding War Diaries and Intelligence Summaries are contained in F.S. Regs., Part II. and the Staff Manual respectively. Title pages will be prepared in manuscript.

Place	Date	Hour	Summary of Events and Information	Remarks and references to Appendices
BEAUCAMP	1 2 3 4 5		Trench Routine.	
	5		Company was relieved on left sector of Divisional front by 60th M.G. Coy. Company relieved 59th M.G. Coy on centre sector of Divisional front.	
GOUZEAU-COURT	5 6 7 8 9 10 11		Trench Routine.	
	12		Company was relieved on centre sector of Divisional front by 59th M.G. Coy. Company relieved 61st M.G. Coy on right sector of Divisional front.	
	13 14 15 16 17 18		Trench Routine.	
			Company was relieved by 35th M.G. Coy on right hand guns & 36th M.G. Coy on left hand guns. Company	

A 5834 Wt.W4973/M637. 750,000 8/16 D.D. & L. Ltd. Forms/C.2118/13.

Army Form C. 2118.

WAR DIARY
or
INTELLIGENCE SUMMARY.
(Erase heading not required.)

Instructions regarding War Diaries and Intelligence Summaries are contained in F. S. Regs., Part II. and the Staff Manual respectively. Title pages will be prepared in manuscript.

Place	Date	Hour	Summary of Events and Information	Remarks and references to Appendices
RAILTON	18		Advance proceeded to RAILTON and spent the night in bivouacs.	
	19		The morning was spent in preparation of guns and equipment for the line. Company proceeded to line at 4 p.m. & took up position at R19 C 90.70 Gouzeaucourt Sheet preparatory to an attack on the morning of 20th inst.	
	20		The Division attacked the enemy on a two Brigade front at 6.20 a.m. The company advanced behind the second wave of tanks at 100 yds interval between sections. No casualties were incurred reaching our objective and during its advance was only molested by a little M.G. fire. The company took up a position about R9 L 30.90 and covered the advance of the infantry to their second objective. Guns ceased fire at 9.55 a.m.
Emplacements were then dug in the shewring	

A 8834 Wt.W4973/M687 750,000 8/16 D. D. & L. Ltd. Forms/C.2118/13.

WAR DIARY or INTELLIGENCE SUMMARY.

(Erase heading not required.)

Army Form C. 2118.

Place	Date	Hour	Summary of Events and Information	Remarks and references to Appendices
	20		Support line in order to consolidate that line and also to put down a defensive barrage	
	21		Remained in present position	
	22		All guns moved to barrage with M.2.c 60.50 and 8 guns and moved for barrage work about M.2.d 10.30. Coy HQ being at gun pits the same gun pits	
	23			
	24			
	25		Remained in same position and fired during the night of many communications	
	26			
	27		Guns moved to position in accordance with Brigade Scheme of Defence. Position of guns being as follows. One section at M.4.d.26.15. One section at M.8.a.50.65. 2 guns about M.7.b.50.50 and 2 guns at R.25.b.70. Forward officer allotted by officer from Hdrs HQ	
	28			
	29			
	30		Enemy attacked our positions considerably in the am	

Army Form C. 2118.

WAR DIARY
or
INTELLIGENCE SUMMARY.

December 1917

(Erase heading not required.)

Place	Date	Hour	Summary of Events and Information	Remarks and references to Appendices
FINS	1.		Details who had proceeded to line on 30th ult. returned about 3pm. No appreciable raid was made by the Company on the line, but along the line retained to near H.Q. 2Lieut. Alard that nobody of the Company had been either taken prisoner or killed. Casualties were total: Returned at 3 Officers missing (Lieut J. Knox-Brown; 2/Lt G. Garth Liff. W.A.P. Wallis) 5 O.R. wounded and 41 O.R. missing.	
"	2.			
"	3.		Awaiting orders to move.	
"	4.		Company left FINS area about 2pm by bus; arrived at YTRES railhead about 3pm. Entrained at YTRES 9pm. Detrained at BUIRE at about 2 a.m. + proceeded to billets at RIBEMONT. Transport left FINS about 11a.m. - halted at end of first days march at MEAULTE.	
RIBEMONT	5.		Company remained in billets. Transport proceeded on march from MEAULTE to ORVILLE.	
"	6.		Company left billets at RIBEMONT at 8 am, entraining at ALBERT at 10 am for BEAURAINVILLE, detraining there about 7pm + marched to billets at TORCY, arriving about 10.30 pm. Transport proceeded on march from ORVILLE to CANTELEUX.	
TORCY	7.		Company at rest in billets. Transport marched on march from CANTELEUX to MARCONELLE.	
"	8.		Company at rest in billets. Transport proceeded on march from MARCONELLE to TORCY, arriving about 3pm.	

WAR DIARY
of
INTELLIGENCE SUMMARY.
(Erase heading not required.)

Army Form C. 2118.

SHEET II

Instructions regarding War Diaries and Intelligence Summaries are contained in F. S. Regs., Part II. and the Staff Manual respectively. Title pages will be prepared in manuscript.

Place	Date	Hour	Summary of Events and Information	Remarks and references to Appendices
TORCY	9		Training	
"	10		2/Lt H.H.J.PRATT. proceeded on leave to U.K.	
"	11		Company embussed at 9am & proceeded to BLARINGHEM cover & occupied billets in BANDRINGHEM. Transport left TORCY at 9 am.	
BANDRING- HEM	12		Transport arrived about 4 pm	
"	13		Company Training. 2/Lieut W Lee Wilson left for U.K. for interview re commission in Indian Army.	
"	14		2/Lieut R.E. NELSON; 2/Lt A.Y.WALLACE; 2/Lt S.WAINE arrived 10½ OR reinforcements arrived from Base	
"	15		Company Training	
"	16		"	
"	17		" 2/Lt N.L. TURTON proceeded on Gas Course.	
"	18		"	
"	19		Company & Transport moved from BANDRINGHEM to RACQUINGHEM.	
RACQUING- HEM	20		Company Training	
	21		2/Lt N.L TURTON & L/Cpl ASTLE arrived from 9th Corps Gas School	
	22		Church Parade for all denominations Capt A.E. ROLLINGS M.C. a DMGO proceeded to 30th Div H.Q with the purpose of being consulted onward the MG Defence of the Line	
	23			

Army Form C. 2118.

WAR DIARY
or
INTELLIGENCE SUMMARY.
(Erase heading not required.)

Place	Date	Hour	Summary of Events and Information	Remarks and references to Appendices
	24		Capt A.E. Rollings M.C. returned from 30th Div H.Q. Company Training	
	25		Christmas Festivities	
	26			
	27.		2/Lt H.H.C. Pratt returned from leave	
	28		2/Lts F.E. Welson & T.S. Waine proceeded to reconnoitre the line. Company Training	
	29.		Company Training	
	30		2/Lt A.Y. Wallace & L/Sgt Curran proceeded to 2nd Army Central School. Bathing Parade	
	31		Training	

27 MG Coy
Vol 11

WAR DIARY
or
INTELLIGENCE SUMMARY. January 1918.

Army Form C. 2118.

Place	Date	Hour	Summary of Events and Information	Remarks and references to Appendices
BACQUING-HEM.	1		Company Training. 2/Lt N.L.TURTON evacuated to Base 31/12/17.	
	2		" Information received that 2/Lt G.GAY was prisoner of war.	
	3		"	
	4		Preparations for move.	
	5		Company moved to forward area. Disembarked at FAULINGHEM about 8.30 am & detrained at DICKEBUSCH about 12 noon. 2/Lt HUTTON, 2/Lt PRATT, 2/Lt NELSON and 2 teams of 'A' Section, 2/Lt BISSON & 4 teams of 'B' Section proceeded to line by light railway and relieved 226 M.G. Coy. (advanced Coy H.Q. STIRLING CASTLE). Remainder of Coy proceeded to billets in DICKEBUSCH.	
DICKEBUSCH	6		2/Lieut R.C.BETTS proceeded on leave to U.K. 2/Lieut N.L.TURTON evacuated to U.K. sick.	
	7		Company near H.Q. & transport moved from DICKEBUSCH to RENINGHURST over (9TIBRA Camp. Sheet 28, M.5.c.2.6.).	
RENINGHURST	8		2/Lieut W.LEE WILSON struck off strength on appointment to Indian Army	
	9		Training & camp fatigues.	
	10		"	

Army Form C. 2118.

WAR DIARY
or
INTELLIGENCE SUMMARY.

(Erase heading not required.)

SHEET II

Place	Date	Hour	Summary of Events and Information	Remarks and references to Appendices
REMINGHURST	11		Lieut GOODING, 2/Lieut SUCKLING and 4 teams of "B" Section of 1 team of "D" Sec proceeded to line by light railway for MG Section relief	
	12		Capt ROLLINGS MC relieved 2/Lt HUTTON in line	
	13		Training & fatigues	
	14			
	16			
	17		2/Lt PRATT DICKINSON and 5 teams of "B" & "C" Secns and 4 teams of "D"Sec proceeded to line by light railway for MG section relief	
	18		2/Lt HUTTON relieved Capt ROLLINGS in line	
	19		Training & fatigues	
	20			
	21		Lieut DL HOWARD MC transferred from 59th MG Coy. assumed command of second in command	
	22		Training & fatigues	
	23		Lieut GOODING, 2/Lieut SUCKLING and 9 teams of "A" and "C" Sections proceeded to line by light railway for MG section relief	O.O. No 2 attached
			2/Lieut RG BETTS rejoined Company from leave.	

Army Form C. 2118.

WAR DIARY
or
INTELLIGENCE SUMMARY.
(Erase heading not required.)

Instructions regarding War Diaries and Intelligence Summaries are contained in F. S. Regs., Part II. and the Staff Manual respectively. Title pages will be prepared in manuscript.

Place	Date	Hour	Summary of Events and Information	Remarks and references to Appendices
RENINGHURST	24		Capt. A.E. ROLLINGS M.C. proceeded on leave to U.K.; Lieut Dr. HOWARD M.B. assumed duties of Commanding Officer during Capt ROLLING's absence. Lieut J.S.GOODING assumed duties of second in command	
			Lieut HOWARD & 2/Lieut BETTS relieved 2/Lt HUTTON and Lieut GOODING respectively in the line	
	25		Training & fatigues.	
	26		" "	
	27		" "	
	28		" 2/Lieut M.S. HUTTON proceeded on leave to U.K.	
	29		2/Lieuts PRATT & 2/Lieut NELSON and 9 teams of 'A' & 'C' Sections proceeded to the line by light railway for public section relief	O.O.N°3 attached
	30		Lieut HOWARD was relieved by Lieut GOODING in the line.	
	31		Training & fatigues.	

J Wearn 2/Lt

for Commanding 217 M.G.Coy

SECRET

217th Machine Gun Coy O.O. No 2.

Map Ref Sh 28 N.E

1. The nine Gun Teams in the line will be relieved by nine Gun Teams from rear H.Q under Lieut J.S. GOODING and 2/Lieut P.H. SUCKLING on 23rd January.

2. The five Gun Teams under Lieut GOODING will relieve five Gun Teams of 2/Lt H.M.J PRATT at FITZCLARENCE FARM

The four Gun Teams under 2/Lt SUCKLING will relieve the four Gun Teams of 2/Lt NELSON at J15 c.30.40.

3. Guides will be at ADVANCED COMPANY H.Q at 12 noon on 23rd January.

4. The relieving teams will entrain at FUZEVILLE (H35 a 6.8.) at 10am 23rd January.

5. A N.C.O. will be detailed to remain at advanced Coy H.Q in order to superintend the issue of rations to Ration Parties at the Dump daily.

6. Section Officers will render a roll of the Gun Teams under their Command at REAR COY H.Q.

7. Advanced Coy H.Q will report 'relief complete' to REAR HQ by wire.

8. On completion of relief the Gun Teams relieved will proceed under Section Officers

– 2 –

to MANOR HALT. Train leaves MANOR HALT at 4.30 pm 23rd January.

9   ACKNOWLEDGE.

January 22nd 1918

D. L. HOWARD. Lieut
for Capt
O.C. 217 M.G. Coy.

217 Machine Gun Coy. O.O. No 3.

Map Ref. 28 N.E. 1/10000

1. Nine gun teams in the line will be relieved in the line by nine teams from rear H.Q. on the 29th inst under Sec.Lieut. PRATT and Sec Lieut. NELSON.

2. Five gun teams under 2/Lt NELSON will relieve the gun teams of 2/Lt BETTS at J14. d. 40.80. The four teams under 2/Lt PRATT will relieve the teams under 2/Lt SUCKLING at the Tower J 15 c 30. 40.

3. Guides (one per team) will be at advanced Coy H.Q.

4. The teams for the relief from rear H.Q will entrain at FUZEVILLE 10 am on day of 29th

5. One N.C.O will relieve Cpl EILBECK at Coy H.Q (if necessary).

6. Rolls of gun teams will be rendered to rear Coy H.Q.

7. Advanced Coy H.Q will report relief complete to Rear H.Q by wire.

8. On completion of relief relieved teams will proceed to MANOR HALT under section arrangements to entrain for Rear H.Q at 4.30 pm

9. ACKNOWLEDGE.

J. S. GOODING. Lieut
for Capt
O.C. 217 M.G. Coy

Army Form C. 2118.

WAR DIARY
INTELLIGENCE SUMMARY.
(Erase heading not required.)

February 1918.

Vol 12

Place	Date	Hour	Summary of Events and Information	Remarks and references to Appendices
RENING-HELST	1		Training and fatigues	
	2		"	
	3		"	
	4		2nd Lieut A.Y. WALLACE rejoined from Course.	O.O. No 4 attached
	5		2nd Lts section relieved by 2/Lt BATTS, 2/Lt WALLACE and nine gun teams	
	6		Training and fatigues. Lieut HOWARD relieved Lieut GOODING in the Line.	
	7		"	
	8		"	
	9		3rd Lt section relieved by 2/Lt SUCKLING, 2/Lt NELSON and nine gun teams	O.O. N.5 attached
	10		Training and fatigues. Lieut GOODING relieved Lieut HOWARD in the Line.	
	11		"	
	12		" 2/Lt HUTTON rejoined the Coy from leave.	
	13		Sections in line were relieved by 247 M.G. Coy (37th Div.).	
	14		Coy left ATSARA Camp 11.15am and entrained at DICKEBUSCH 1.30pm, Coy detrained at EBBINGHEM about 4pm and marched to billets in BLARINGHEM.	
	15		Transport left ATSARA Camp about 5.30am for BLARINGHEM, staying for one night in STRAZEELE area.	
	16		Coy. Sgt. Major EVANS W.T. joined Coy from 204 M.G. Coy.	B.H.

Army Form C. 2118.

SHEET II

WAR DIARY
INTELLIGENCE SUMMARY.
(Erase heading not required.)

Place	Date	Hour	Summary of Events and Information	Remarks and references to Appendices
BLARING-HEM	17		Transport arrived from STRAZEELE area about 1pm.	
	18		Coy training.	
	19		" "	
	20		Coy, comp ex and transport left BLARING HEM 6.30pm and marched to STEENBECQUE entraining there about 10pm.	O.O. No 6 attached
	21		Coy detrained at NESLE about 12 noon and marched to billets in ESMERY HALLON arriving about 5pm.	
ESMERY-HALLON	22		Coy training.	
	23		Coy, comple with transport left ESMERY HALLON 1.30 p.m. and marched to billets in MARGNY arriving about 5 p.m. Coy. H.Q. Bosche House (Tq.d. 80.90 Sheet 66D).	
MARGNY	24		Coy. training	
	25		" "	
	26		" "	
	27		" "	
	28		2/Lieut. A.Y. WALLACE proceeded on leave to U.K. Coy. training. Capt. A.E. ROLLINGS M.C. rejoined the Coy. from leave to U.K.	

for Capt. D. Howard Lt
Commanding 217 M.G. Coy

SECRET.

217 Machine Gun Coy — O.O. No 4

Map Ref Sheet 28 NE 1/10,000.

1. The nine Gun Teams now in the line will be relieved by nine Gun Teams from rear H.Q on the 4th Feb. 1918, under 2/Lt BETTS and 2nd Lt WALLACE.

2. The five Gun Teams under 2/Lt WALLACE will relieve the Five Gun Teams under 2/Lt NELSON at J14 d.40.80. The four Gun Teams under 2/Lt BETTS will relieve the four Gun Teams under 2/Lt PRATT at the TOWER J.15 c.30.40

3. One guide per Gun Team will be at advanced Coy H.Q at 4.30pm, 4th inst, to guide the relieving teams to Gun positions.

4. The relieving teams from rear H.Q will entrain at FUZEVILLE at 3pm on the 4th inst.

5. Arrangements will be made, if necessary, to relieve the N.C.O at advanced Coy. H.Q.

6. Section Officers of relieving teams will render a roll of their Gun Teams to rear Coy H.Q before proceeding to the line.

7. Advanced Coy H.Q will report 'relief complete' to rear Coy H.Q by wire.

8. On completion of relief, relieved teams will proceed to MANOR HALT under Section arrangements to entrain for rear H.Q at 7.30pm, 4th inst.

9. ACKNOWLEDGE.

3/2/18.

S. Warin 2/Lt
for Commdg 217 M.G.Coy

SECRET

<u>217 Machine Gun Coy - O.O. No 4</u>
    <u>Amendment No 1.</u>   <u>Map. Ref. Sh. 28 NE. 1/10,000</u>

<u>1</u>   In para. 4, for FUZEVILLE read ZEVECOTEN.

<u>2</u>   In para. 8, line 2, for MANOR HALT read LAMBTON & in line 3, for 7.30 pm read 8 pm.

<u>3</u>   ACKNOWLEDGE

4/2/18.

                           S. Waini 2/Lt
                     for Commdg 217 M.G. Coy

SECRET

214 Machine Gun Coy — O.O. No 5

Map Ref Sheet 28 NE 1/10,000

1. The nine Gun Teams now in the line will be relieved by nine Gun Teams from rear HQ on the 9th Feb. 1918., under 2/Lt SUCKLING and 2/Lt NELSON.

2. The five Gun Teams under 2/Lt SUCKLING will relieve the five Gun Teams under 2/Lt WALLACE at J14.d.40.80. The four Gun Teams under 2/Lt NELSON will relieve the four Gun Teams under 2/Lt BETTS at VERBOEK & CARLISLE Farms and J10.c.

3. One guide per Gun Team will be at advanced Coy H.Q. at 6.0 pm, 9th inst to guide the relieving teams to Gun positions.

4. The relieving teams from rear H.Q will entrain at FUZEVILLE at 4 pm on the 9th inst.

5. Section Officers of relieving teams will render a roll of their Gun Teams to rear Coy H.Q before proceeding to the line.

6. Advanced Coy H.Q will report 'relief complete' by the code word LEMON to rear Coy H.Q by wire.

7. On completion of relief, relieved teams will proceed to MANOR HALT under section arrangements to entrain for rear H.Q at 1 am, 10th inst.

8. ACKNOWLEDGE.

Jas Hooding Lt.

Comndg 217 M.G. Coy.

21st M.G. Coy.   O.O. No. 6

1. The Coy. complete with transport will entrain at STEENBECQUE Station on the night of the 20th/21st February 1918 and detrain at NESLE.

2. The Coy. will parade at 6.15 p.m. 20/2/18 to march off at 6.30 p.m. and will march to the Station to be there three hours before the train moves off. The train departs 12.10 a.m. 21/2/18.

3. There will be a loading party of the 11th R.Bs to assist in entraining transport and an unloading party of the 2nd Scottish Rifles to assist in detraining.

4. A lorry will call at Coy. H.Q. which is at the disposal of the Coy. One half of blanket per man, Officers Mess Kit, 12 Dixies and ration of tea sugar and milk will be loaded on the lorry. A loading party of L/C. Ievrey and six men will remain behind to load the lorry + will proceed on the lorry to entraining station.

5. Trains. The train consists of one officers coach, seventeen flat trucks, and thirty covered trucks. Each flat truck will take an average of four axles. Each covered truck forty men, or 8 L.D. Horses or mules.
   No personnel or stores will be allowed in the brake vans at each end of the train or on the roofs of the trucks.

6. Entrainment of the Coy. must be complete half an hour before the time of departure of train.

7. Breast ropes for horses will be provided by the Coy.

8. All doors of covered trucks + carriages on the right hand side of the train when on the main line are to be kept closed.

9. Water carts will travel full, water bottles will be filled and horses watered before leaving.

10. No man is allowed to detrain without permission after entrainment.

11) The train is to be left perfectly clean in all respects.

12) All mens' blankets will be rolled in tens and carried to the Orderly Room and dumped.

13) <u>Dress</u>. Full marching order, jerkins to be worn under tunics, steel helmets strapped on back of pack, canteen slung on supporting straps underneath packs.

14) Billets are to be perfectly cleaned by 5 p.m.

15. ACKNOWLEDGE

W. S. Hutton 2/Lt.

Comdg. 31st M.G. Coy.